Widening the Circle

Designing Worship
That Reaches

Augsburg Fortress

Minneapolis

WIDENING THE CIRCLE
Designing Worship That Reaches

Developed in cooperation with the Division for Congregational Ministries of the Evangelical Lutheran Church in America, Richard Webb, project manager.

Editors: Andrea Lee Schieber and James Satter

Cover design by David Meyer
Text design by James Satter
Cover art copyright © 2001, PhotoDisc, Inc.
Interior illustrations by Brian Jensen, Studio Arts

ISBN 0-8066-4253-X

Manufactured in the U.S.A.

05   04   03   02   01   1   2   3   4   5   6   7   8   9   10

Contents

CHAPTER 1

Great Commission Basics

Louis R. Forney

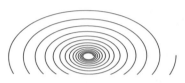

On a busy afternoon I reached across my desk to answer the phone and heard the voice of Ron Hall inviting me out to lunch. He said he wanted to talk to me about something of eternal importance. Just a few months before, Ron had joined the church where I serve as pastor. He was buying lunch, and I said yes.

His story was something he shared easily. In earlier conversations, Ron had told me that he had not been to church since he was a teenager. More than thirty years had passed since he had attended any church regularly. He had tried returning to church a few times, but only on occasion. Recent health problems had nudged him back. Ron felt some guilt about that, but said he somehow knew that coming back to church for what he called a bad reason was better than not coming at all. He said he wasn't sure what he was looking for, but he knew that when he went to church things simply didn't connect.

When they slow down, many people feel the need to connect at some level. Ron had been about to give up going to church a couple years before when he was invited to King of kings. There, he was able to connect to

---

Louis R. Forney is the developer and senior pastor of King of kings Lutheran Church in Shelby Township, Michigan. In ten years, King of kings has grown from a congregation of forty to having more than 1,200 baptized members.

other people and to God. He moved cautiously, trying us on for the right fit for almost a year before joining our congregation. Ron worshiped every Sunday, sitting on the left-hand side near the windows. He was quiet, polite, and easy to talk with.

Ron and I arrived at the restaurant at the same time. After a bit of polite chitchat, Ron told me two things, which he stated rather matter-of-factly. First, he wanted me to know that his health had taken a turn for the worse and that he did not have long to live. Second, he wanted to thank me that he could face his death with peace and he wanted me to know why. He told me how he came to where he was, a story I want to share with you.

Moving from simply not connecting to God to being connected to God and to other people. What a trip! The stakes are incredibly high, not just for Ron, but for millions like him. They want to be connected. Their quality of life now and their eternal life are in the balance. In ways we do not intend and in more ways we do not even know, the church often makes it hard for people to connect. One reason this book has been written is to help all of us see how we can help people like Ron get connected by making more accessible the richer life they seek.

Ron had a fascinating story to share with me. With incredible attention to detail, he retraced his steps back to church. We had a delightful two-hour conversation in the restaurant. Ten days after our lunch together, I proclaimed the good news of the resurrection at his funeral. He knew it was coming. Ron died well. No doubt Jesus intended that when he first commissioned his followers with their job.

We can help people like Ron get connected by making more accessible the richer life they seek.

What is a Great Commission congregation?

Jesus' words to his followers prior to his ascension are referred to as the Great Commission: "Go therefore and make disciples of all nations, baptizing them in the name of the Father and of the Son and of the Holy Spirit, and teaching them to obey everything that I have commanded you. And remember, I am with you always, to the end of the age" (Matthew 28:19-20).

What does it mean to be a Great Commission congregation? It is not just a matter of listening to the Great Commission, or thinking it is a good idea, or even agreeing with it. A Great Commission congregation makes the

See CD
Resource
1A

needed decisions and takes the steps, so the Great Commission becomes reality. The most important thing we do is to widen the circle and help people connect with Jesus.

Here's a personalized translation of the Great Commission: "Help Ron come to know and follow Jesus." The companion CD-ROM includes a Bible study to help you and others in your congregation dig deeper into this familiar passage from Matthew's Gospel.

How do we widen the circle? The focus of this book and CD-ROM is on evangelistic worship—the form and style and substance of worship that reaches. Evangelistic worship is only one, albeit extremely important, quality of a Great Commission congregation. These congregations ask: How do we create a climate that cares more about people like Ron than anything else? How do we help Ron become the most important person in the congregation—before he is even there for the first time? The first step is getting an accurate picture of the people we are reaching out to.

Dorothy, it's not Kansas anymore!

There was a time when folks lived in what has been called a church-going society. Just a few decades ago, some mortgage loan applications required you to list your church membership and the name of your pastor as a reference in order to apply for a loan. The question was not "Do you go to church?" but "What church do you attend?" While change has come fast in most facets of society in the last several decades, it is obvious to most church observers, as it was to Dorothy in *The Wizard of Oz,* that it's not Kansas anymore!

Historically, the church has crafted its message for believers. The great stained-glass windows of European cathedrals shared the Christian message with people who already knew it. Many worship services are designed for insiders. Many musical styles and liturgies used in worship preserve the past instead of relating to the present. Since 1950, mainline denominations have seen significant membership decline. At the same time, half of the people in most communities do not have a church home. In some areas that number runs 70 percent and higher (*Counting Flocks and Lost Sheep: Trends in Religious Preference Since World War II,*

Tom W. Smith, National Opinion Research Center, University of Chicago, GSS Social Change Report No. 26, February 1988, revised January 1991). We're not doing a very good job of reaching most people. It's not Kansas anymore!

People now come to church with a different set of needs and expectations. They are asking a different set of questions than they used to ask. A generation ago, a label was coined that describes these new folks— "seekers."

Most churches are best at telling the gospel to people who already know it. Congregations like Willow Creek Community Church in suburban Chicago have helped many churches become more sensitive to seekers: people who are looking for some answers, but don't know about God's word.

In recent years, a new phenomenon has appeared in our society. More and more people cannot yet be described as seekers. They are not looking for answers or even asking questions. At the least, they are not asking questions of the church. For one reason or another, these "pre-seekers" have decided that church is not the place to look for answers. How does the church fulfill the Great Commission when we have trouble communicating with seekers and we can't even get pre-seekers to talk to us? Ron had been trying to ask questions of the church and was not getting workable answers he could apply to his life. He was about to give up because of the barriers in place, no one in the church cared.

The first step in reaching many people today is helping them see that we care.

Something deep down inside me weeps when people like Ron conclude that the church doesn't care. The church does care. Most Christians are good people who care about others and want to meet their needs. But many of us don't know how to connect with our neighbors and tell them about Jesus. We don't know how to communicate our care in a way that makes sense to outsiders. The first step in reaching many people today is helping them see that we care; that our actions line up with our words.

Ron saw people who were willing to help his daughter through a crisis. When he looked closer, he saw people in a church that carried out a dozen acts of kindness because they seemed to genuinely care. It was an act of evangelism. He saw people living out the love of Christ. That caught his attention and sparked his curiosity.

Invitational evangelism

70 to 80
percent of
people who
come to
church
responded to
the invitation
of a friend
or family
member.

Ron had now noticed the church. He didn't know where the building was, but he knew something about the people who were a part of the church. They cared about other people—people they did not know. These folks had integrity and genuineness. He wanted to know more. A small foundation had been laid for Ron.

The times Ron had been invited to church in the last thirty years, he was suspicious of some ulterior motive. Anything that resembled evangelism always felt more focused on the needs of the church than on the needs of Ron. The church always seemed to want his money. Ron needed to hear an invitation that held some promise that the church might meet him where he was.

One of the most effective starting points for reaching people is simple invitational evangelism. Studies that look at how people end up in church tend to point in the same direction. For example, 70 to 80 percent of people who come to church responded to the invitation of a friend or family member (*Church and Denominational Growth,* C. Kirk Hadaway and David Roozen, Abingdon, 1993, pp. 129-130). Ron had encountered some people he trusted at King of kings and was open. Inviting people to worship is perhaps the most effective evangelism strategy available.

The problem is that most mainline Christians don't do a lot of inviting. Perhaps it has to do with how they think their friends might experience their church. The gospel is there, but it can be hard for an outsider to hear. Regularly scheduled Friendship Weekends are an effective way to increase the number of invitations that members offer to friends and relatives. A brief outline for Friendship Weekend has been included on the CD-ROM. Scheduling two or three Friendship Weekends each year can increase the response rate. Often the people extending the most enthusiastic invitations are the newest members who first attended because of the invitation of a friend.

See CD
Resource
1B

Hospitality

For a congregation to successfully reach others, what happens next is crucial. If unchurched people attend, what will they find when they arrive?

That determines whether they come back. Congregational hospitality is sometimes difficult to pin down and define, but you know it when you feel it. Good hospitality has some objective elements. Can people find a place to park their car and figure out which door to come through? Is the building attractive? Does anyone talk to them when they get inside? Are there signs that help them find their way around? Can they follow the worship service?

Good hospitality also has some subjective elements. Are people genuine? Is the atmosphere comfortable? Do the nonverbal cues give a warm feeling? Some people argue that a good feeling in a worshiper should not be our highest goal. While in theory this is true, we still have to get people in the door and we have to provide something that will help them decide to come back. If we don't, we have lost an opportunity. Where we think people ought to be is less important than where they actually are. Jesus met people where they were. Great Commission congregations design worship and evangelism to meet people where they are.

The CD-ROM includes a hospitality survey you may use to conduct a self-assessment. Accurate information about the experience of first-time guests is a helpful diagnostic tool. If part of the purpose of worship is to experience the presence of God, are people able to do that? The church often puts up so many barriers that a high-hurdler would be prevented from hearing the gospel. Improving our hospitality quotient helps people make the needed connections.

Not long ago I was blessed with a vacation to Germany and had the opportunity to worship at the Castle Church in Wittenberg where Martin Luther posted the Ninety-five Theses that sparked the Protestant Reformation. There were a few words of welcome in English, but then we endured a ninety-minute worship service entirely in German. Being familiar with worship patterns, I could identify some basic parts of the service, but most of the time I was completely lost. I tried to act interested, while feeling totally disconnected. What disturbed me was what I saw as I looked around the church. Most German-speaking people seemed to be just as lost as I was. Is that what it is like for people when they worship in my church or your church on Sunday morning? Do they hear us welcome them in English and proceed to do everything else in a language they don't understand?

Great Commission congregations design worship and evangelism to meet people where they are.

See CD Resource 1C

After the worship service ends, we ask that members talk to someone they do not know.

Many people going to a church think their church is warm and friendly and their service is easy to follow. Most first-time worshipers would beg to differ. It is difficult to get an accurate picture of what our own church is like. Interviewing first-time worshipers will help you find out what worship was like for them. Newcomers can see things you no longer see about yourself. They can identify your barriers better than you can and they will help you take an honest look at your hospitality. Interviews with guests have helped us at King of kings learn a lot over the years:

- Greeters at the door are not as important to guests as we had thought. They come across like "paid" nice people.
- Coffee and juice can help open a conversation and give a reason for staying. But if guests have to hunt for the coffee and juice, our effort at hospitality, unfortunately, doesn't count.
- How we treat children is critical. The nursery is very important to parents of young children.
- We don't see the "church junk" around the building, but newcomers do.
- Conversations going on in the lobby between people set much of the tone for the newcomer.
- Restrooms are important. If the restrooms are dirty or if something is out of order, guests will get a negative impression of the congregation.

There are also a few "lobby rules" at King of kings that Ron found helpful. He was not consciously aware of any of them, but they helped his initial experiences be very positive.

First, we call the entryway a "lobby" and not a "narthex." We use language that will make sense to people who are new to church.

Second, we ask people to follow the "two-minute rule." For the first two minutes after the worship service ends, we ask that members talk to someone they do not know.

Third, we ask that congregation members avoid what we affectionately call "holy huddles." Members often stand around talking with their backsides to the rest of the world.

Fourth, we ask leaders to operate like business is closed on Sunday. Let's not talk to each other about church business, but rather tend to the more important business on Sunday between services—helping newcomers feel at home. These practices operating behind the scenes helped Ron hear the gospel.

What is worship that reaches?

In recent years, much energy has gone into debates about worship styles. This book is aimed at helping congregational leaders create a worship experience where people come into the presence of God, where they can hear the gospel of Jesus Christ. That is more important than whether you use certain musical instruments. When worship does not speak to the guest, a Great Commission congregation has failed.

Worship that reaches is contextual and creates connections

The question of worship style is one that is best answered in a local context. There is nothing inherently "right" or "wrong" about a given worship style or format. In the community around King of kings, most residents have some church background from childhood but rejected church in their teens because it seemed irrelevant. When a congregation offers something that looks like the experience people left in their childhood, they want to leave again. Then we never get a chance to communicate the gospel. Ron told me that he left the church for a reason, and most of the congregations he attended as an adult looked like what he left. He did not want to go back. Ron's views reflect that of many people in this area.

Great Commission congregations design their worship to attract unchurched people in their community. Worship that reaches is contextual and creates connections with other people and with God. You know you have worship that reaches when worshipers return next week and decide to keep coming.

Getting involved in the life of the church

After Ron came to church he noticed that we noticed him. Intentional follow-up has been a key to reaching people at King of kings. We believe that if someone takes time to come to us, we're coming back at them. While our approach is low-key, the average first-time guest will receive a typed letter from the church office and a hand-written note from a member of the congregation. We also try to visit them at home before three days pass, and we put their name on the mailing list and it stays there unless the visitor asks to be removed from the list.

We know that some folks connect fast, while others are slow to connect to a congregation. We want them to know that we're glad they came and we want to invite them to come back. One of the keys for us has been including a Response Form in our worship folder that allows anyone to get connected to anything happening in our church. See CD-ROM Resource 1D for more information.

See CD Resource 1D

Membership and discipleship

One of the things Ron said he appreciated was that it was easy to become a member of King of kings. We do not try to teach someone everything about the faith before they join the congregation. The whole Christian life is aimed at making disciples, so we don't need to finish the task during the membership class. In Acts 8, when the new convert enthusiastically wanted to be baptized, Philip did not send him to a lengthy class. He baptized him. Ron needed to start out with a low commitment and take baby steps to grow from there.

In many mainline churches, it seems we have tended to raise the barriers to membership—making it hard to join—and have lowered the standards of membership—so it means little to belong. Instead, we can lower the barriers so people get connected, and then work to raise the standards of membership. Enlist the believer in a lifelong journey of growth and discipleship. Ron decided he wanted to join the church and "get going." The membership class was designed to help Ron learn what it means to be a follower of Jesus Christ: a disciple. We clearly communicated to Ron the faith practices that would help him grow as a disciple and become a mature believer. We call those faith practices the Marks of Discipleship and they are included in our Values, Mission, and Vision statement, which can be found on the CD-ROM.

See CD Resource 1E

We have been called to help Ron come to know and follow Jesus. Borrowing from the leaders of Willow Creek, lost people matter to God and therefore they matter to us. As we widen the circle to reach out with the gospel of Jesus Christ, we can make it easier for people like Ron to come in. Worship designed to communicate the gospel is a critical goal for Great Commission congregations. God has placed in the heart of all people a desire to hear the gospel. What are we doing that helps them hear it? What are we doing that is getting in the way? What will it cost us to make the changes needed to reach them?

Toward the end of our lunch that day Ron told me his greatest satisfaction was that a few months earlier his unchurched wife, Jan, had responded to his invitation to worship. He knew she would be with him in eternity someday.

CHAPTER 2

A Faithful Course for Worship

Bob McIntyre

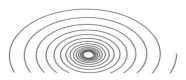

Winds of change are blowing through the worship practice of churches across North America. An ever-widening circle of congregations and denominations is feeling the impact. You may be part of it.

In a fast-growing community west of Portland, Oregon, three mission churches recently began—a Baptist church, a Lutheran church, and a Methodist church. All three churches are employing new technologies and contemporary arts to reach a population of unconvinced but spiritually receptive people. The same community is home to long-established congregations. Worship schedules offer a menu of times and styles. Signs of innovation leap into view: projection screens flank the cross and communion table, worship bands lead corporate song in the shadow of the pipe organ.

Not all embrace the change taking place in worship today. Some see the Spirit of God at work and want to seize every opportunity to reach people for Christ. Others raise flags of caution and fear the loss of cherished traditions. They, too, want to reach people for Christ but sense the spirit of this age at work—a spirit enamored by growth in numbers whatever the cost.

Bob McIntyre is a pastor serving Community of Christ Church in Hillsboro, Oregon, a new congregation of the Evangelical Lutheran Church in America.

What in God's name is guiding us?

Will our worship practice merely be a market enterprise or a missionary endeavor guided by the Spirit of God? As was the case when the apostle Paul left port on his first missionary journey, the waters ahead of us are uncharted. Paul could not foresee the impact his mission work would have on the worship traditions he had known. Neither can we. A faithful biblical and theological compass is needed to guide our worship practice and the process of change.

This chapter begins with a look at a biblical vision of worship then moves to the Protestant reformers of the sixteenth century to highlight the priorities that guided their renewal of worship and the practical outcomes that followed. Our context today and the practical steps we can take to foster a worship life that is faithful to the gospel and to our mission in Christ conclude this chapter.

Authentic worship is grounded in the saving acts and activity of God.

A biblical vision of worship

In the Bible we encounter diverse worship practices spanning centuries and crossing cultures. Current conversations about worship that reaches often center on what we do, from music styles to message series. The Bible directs our eyes to God—what God is doing and for whom God is doing it.

Responding to the God who saves

At the heart of biblical worship is the God who saves. Whatever the setting, authentic worship is grounded in the saving acts and activity of God.

The watershed events of the Bible illustrate the following.

- The Exodus-Mount Sinai experience is the centerpiece of Old Testament faith and worship life. The people of Israel were set free by God's power, gathered in worship around God's word, and called to life in covenant with God (Exodus 3:12, 24:1-8; Deuteronomy 7:7-9). Generations to follow participated in worship not only to celebrate God's mighty acts of yesterday but to experience God's promises and saving power today (Psalm 103:1-5), and they responded with prayer, praise, and faithful lives.

**God's vision
for worship
extends
beyond those
already
present.**

• For the New Testament church the decisive events of salvation are
the death and resurrection of Jesus Christ. In Christ God had taken
a stunning new initiative and was revealed to be one in three:
Father, Son, and Holy Spirit (Romans 5:1-4, 8). In worship, the early
Christian community proclaimed the gospel—God's saving word—
and participated in God's saving work through baptism, the Lord's
Supper, and common prayer (Acts 2:42; Romans 1:16; Romans 6:3-4;
1 Corinthians 10:16-17). They believed God's Spirit was active in their
midst to call, to convict, to awaken faith, and to fill hearts with
a fresh outpouring of God's gifts (1 Corinthians 12:4-11, 14:26-32).

• A biblical vision of worship begins with God. Whatever the particular
worship traditions and practices of a congregation, the guiding light of
everything that happens is worship is God and God's redemptive
work. The Bible invites us to believe that in worship God is both
present and moving with power for us—yet not for believers alone.

Reaching out to all people

When God draws the worship circle, God circles the globe. God's vision
for worship extends beyond those already present. We see it in the Old
Testament. We are called to do something about it in the body of Christ
today.

Passages in the Old Testament point to a worship life that includes both
believers and seekers. The worship instructions of Israel envision the participation of "aliens" or foreigners (Numbers 15:14; Deuteronomy 26:2,
11). The picture expands with the prophets. Nations would stream to
Jerusalem to "proclaim the praise of the LORD" (Isaiah 60:6, also 55:5);
people of every language would come because they had heard "God is
with you" (Zechariah 8:22-23, also 2:11).

When the risen Christ passed the torch of the gospel to his church the
vision of the prophets took a divine twist. The nations would not need to
stream to Jerusalem. Instead, Jesus sent his followers to the nations
(Matthew 28:18-20; Acts 1:8).

To cross the divide of culture and faith, the apostle Paul broke with
long-held tradition that separated Jews and Gentiles. Paul formed commu-

nities of faith and worship suited to the Gentile culture he served. His work met with resistance from the Jewish Christian community. Paul insisted on the truth and freedom of the gospel and received the affirmation of the apostles and elders in Jerusalem who, in his own words, "asked only that we remember the poor" (Galatians 2:1-14; cf. Acts 15:1-29). His letters also make clear: the doors of worship were open to believers and seekers. He instructed the church in Corinth to adjust its worship practice for the sake of nonbelievers (1 Corinthians 14:23-24). Paul portrayed a worship life in which the gospel is communicated with clarity so a seeker, struck to the heart, "will bow down before God and worship him, declaring, 'God is really among you'" (1 Corinthians 14:25).

God is among us—creating communities of worship where God moves with power through the gospel and all are welcomed to respond through faith in Jesus Christ. In the pioneering work of Paul this biblical vision of worship in action is clear. The sixteenth-century Protestant reformers were another group of pioneers who worked to renew the worship of the church.

A look at the Protestant reformers

The leaders of the Protestant Reformation launched one of the most far-reaching ventures of worship transformation in the history of the church. Like the apostle Paul, they breached walls of language, culture, and tradition. John Calvin, John Huss, Martin Luther, and others sought to recover the heart of Christian worship. Their work has important implications for our time, too.

A new orientation

The rediscovery of the gospel led to a reorientation of worship that emphasized its gospel center. Trends in medieval theology and popular religious practice had led to a common understanding of the Mass as a human work offered to gain a measure of God's grace. The reformers retained the essential pattern of word and sacrament worship but brought the gospel back to its center—God's saving word and work for us proclaimed with the voice, celebrated in the sacraments, and received without measure through the gift of faith in Christ. This reorientation of Christian worship spurred a dramatic course of change in worship practice.

Guiding priorities

In navigating the process of change, the reformers employed several key biblical priorities. Specific changes exhibited distinct theological perspectives, yet they shared a common aim: faithfulness to the witness of God's word and to the mission of Christ.

Faithfulness to the gospel: The prevailing biblical priority guiding the reform of worship was faithfulness to the gospel. The sixteenth-century reformers believed that they stood before a generation that did not know the gospel. Public worship became the front line for the gospel's work to convert human hearts and teach people to lead a Christian life. As Martin Luther wrote in the preface of his new German worship service, "we prepare such orders not for those who already are Christians; . . . such orders are needed for those who are still becoming Christians or need to be strengthened," and further, "For such, one must sing, read, preach, write, and compose. And if it would help matters along, I would have all the bells pealing, and all the organs playing, and have everything ring that can make a sound" (*Luther's Works,* vol. 53, Fortress Press, 1965, p. 62). In worship both evangelism and discipleship were vital dimensions. The standard for worship practices, whatever the particular forms, was set: they must be faithful to the gospel.

Freedom: A second biblical priority operative in the work of the reformers was freedom. Like Paul, the reformers would exercise the freedom of the gospel even if it meant breaking with centuries-old traditions. Here the leaders of the Lutheran movement made a distinction between unity in the essentials of faith and freedom in human custom and practice. In the Augsburg Confession they stressed, "It is not necessary for the true unity of the Christian church that ceremonies, instituted by [people], should be observed uniformly in all places" (*The Book of Concord*, Fortress Press, 1959, p. 32). In evangelical freedom, the reformers crafted new worship orders and practices that reflected their gospel convictions. They also waved a flag of caution.

Love: A third biblical priority of Martin Luther and other Protestant reformers was the law of love. We are free in the gospel, but our freedom is always to be guided by the love of Christ (Romans 14; 1 Corinthians 9: 19-23). In the reform of worship the law of love cut two ways. On the one hand, it called for care and patience in the process and pace of change. Both Calvin and Luther had little tolerance for arbitrary or abrupt change. On the other hand, the same law of love called for reform to move forward. Love for Christ, love for people without the gospel, motivated them to take action.

The practical impact

The challenge of reaching their generation with the gospel propelled the reformers into a dynamic process of change in worship. To bring home the gospel they published new worship orders, composed new sacred song, championed biblical preaching, and provided fresh translations of the scriptures. Traditional forms were simplified and revised. The worship experience was made accessible and adapted to meet the needs of local contexts. Luther's approach in Wittenberg opens a window to the practical dimension of their work.

In a town populated with Latin students and a full range of German people, Luther implemented two kinds of worship services and proposed a third. On Sunday people could attend either a revised Latin service or a German service, developed for the general public. Luther encouraged preachers to speak in a "plain, childlike, popular, and simple way" (*Luther's Works,* vol. 54, Fortress Press, 1967, p. 384). He called on poets and musicians to compose new worship songs and contributed his own. Luther also pictured a third kind of service he did not have time to pursue. He envisioned house churches where small groups of devout Christians would meet for worship to pray, to grow in God's word, even to celebrate the sacraments together.

In the process of change, the reformers sought to be faithful to a biblical vision of worship and to be guided by gospel-centered priorities. The challenge tapped their best energies and insights. They in turn called on the gifts and tools of musicians, poets, artists, and others. What emerged was a worship life that communicated the gospel with fresh power to the people of their time and place. The reformers struggled with the changes and diversity in worship practice that developed but pressed on. As Luther wrote, "we must dare something in the name of Christ" (*Luther's Works,* vol. 53, Fortress Press, 1965, p. 19). Almost five centuries later, so must we.

> "We must dare something in the name of Christ."
> —*Martin Luther*

The context today

Warehouse 242 is not a traditional name for a church, nor is the worship practice of this congregation typical for many mainline Protestant congregations. Based in Charlotte, North Carolina, the church sprang from a Saturday-night worship service for young adults at a local Presbyterian congregation. Worship is open to all, and seekers are called "normal people." Music reflects the sound of contemporary rock bands like Third Day and Creed. Messages are biblical and tackle the life issues of young adults in a post-Christian culture. Of the 450 people who now attend—including a growing number of teenagers and older adults—more than 80 percent have signed on to participate in small groups. The aim in all they do is to "stay true to the gospel." In the process, Warehouse 242 is widening the circle of worship and making new followers of Christ.

Every congregation today faces the task of communicating the gospel faithfully and effectively—and in a mission field of diverse cultures and generational groups. The work of Warehouse 242 is one example of how local churches are responding with creativity and passion. This context for mission holds both opportunities and tensions. On the CD-ROM you will find a small group study on the topic of worship and mission that your can use to explore ideas for and opportunities in your setting.

See CD
Resource
2A

Worship opportunities

Taking cues from the apostle Paul as well as the sixteenth-century reformers, the church has two invaluable opportunities for reaching people through worship today. The first lies in the people God has called and gifted for ministry. The Spirit is raising up a new generation of mission-minded teachers and preachers, evangelists, musicians, songwriters, and artisans.

A second opportunity lies in the resources God has placed at our fingertips. Paul had the Roman roads, and the Protestant reformers had the printing press. We have new technologies and tools of communication. The scriptures call us to be good stewards of God's manifold grace and to employ the gifted people and resources God has given (1 Peter 4:10-11).

Worship tensions

As congregational leaders pursue opportunities for new worship, the tensions that arise around changes in worship practice also need to be addressed. Tensions can flare over custom and style, such as the kind of instruments or music we use. They can also involve matters of faith and substance:

- Is our worship God-centered and true to the gospel?
- Do worship and evangelism go hand in hand?

Informed by a biblical vision of worship and guided by evangelical priorities, we can work through the tensions and move toward a faithful response. As the apostle Paul and the sixteenth-century reformers affirmed, our unity lies in the essentials of our faith. We are free in the gospel to adapt our worship practice to reach people for Christ. How then do we proceed? "Exploring Tensions in Worship" on the CD-ROM is reflection designed to help groups discuss these issues.

See CD Resource 2D

The process of change

Change or adaptation in worship is not a matter of trying the latest trends or techniques. It is a matter of careful, healthy process and faithfulness to the gospel. The process starts with prayer and reflection to work out a common vision for reaching people in our local context. Exploring practical options and developing a course of action follow. Finally, the process calls for consistent, ongoing evaluation.

Getting to the same page

As we consider change in worship for the sake of mission, a first task is to develop a shared vision and plan.

Church leaders can begin by looking at their congregation:

- What is our mission and present make-up?
- What is our vision for worship and outreach?

Leaders also need to gain a picture of the local community:

- Who are the people in our mission field?
- Who is God calling us to reach?
- What are the implications for our worship practice?

CD Resource 2E, "Worship and the Mission Field," is designed for discussing and answering these questions in a small group.

Time needs to be taken to reflect on a biblical vision of worship and to apply the gospel priorities evident in the work of Paul and the reformers. Use CD Resource 2B, "A Biblical Vision for Worship and Outreach," and CD Resource 2C, "Guiding Priorities for Worship That Reaches Out." As leaders consult with the people of the church, addressing tensions and exploring opportunities, a common vision and course of action emerge. "A Process and Plan of Action," CD Resource 2F suggests steps to follow and tasks to include.

See CD Resources

Practical plans

The plans we develop need to be indigenous to our local churches and contexts. Common approaches include incorporating new elements in a traditional service or adding a contemporary service. Some churches are introducing worship services designed in music and style for particular generation groups. Still others are going a step further. Instead of adapting or adding a worship service, they are starting new mission churches with a distinct worship life to reach people in their communities. In each case, we have a rich Christian heritage and wealth of new worship resources to draw on. Different settings, gifts, and resources will lead to different courses of action.

It is not enough simply to ask whether a song is workable or numbers are increasing.

The piece we often miss

Every course of action calls for careful assessment. It is not enough simply to ask whether a song is workable or numbers are increasing. We need to hold what we do accountable to a biblical vision of worship and to the gospel.

Evaluation takes place before and after worship and involves both the worship planner and the worshiper. See CD Resource 2G, "Faithfulness in Worship Planning and Evaluation." Build into your planning and assessment questions that move beyond practical concerns:

See CD Resource 2G

- Does this reflect God's word and vision for life?
- Is worship not only calling people to respond in faith but fostering lives faithful to Christ?

- As we explore mission field forms of worship, we also need to ask mission field questions and incorporate feedback from worshipers.
- Who are we reaching?
- What is their experience of worship and its impact in their lives?

Responses can be gathered through worship evaluation forms given to people on a regular basis. See CD Resource 2H, "Worship Response Form." Occasional focus groups are another avenue and offer deeper interaction and assessment. CD Resource 2I "Worship Focus Group" includes questions to ask. This kind of ongoing evaluation enables us to weigh what we are doing and to adjust course when needed. Whatever evaluation resources or tools are used, the aim is to provide worship services that are effective in reaching people for Christ and faithful to the Lord whose gospel we proclaim.

See CD Resources

A great Savior

In the late nineteenth century, a group of people traveled to England and decided to hear two of the renowned preachers of the day: Joseph Parker and Charles Haddon Spurgeon. They first went to Parker's church and concluded, "Without a doubt, Joseph Parker is the greatest preacher in all the world." With limited time in London, they almost skipped the visit to Spurgeon's church but decided to go. Emerging from the worship service they said, "Without a doubt, Jesus Christ is the greatest Savior in all the world."

Like Christian generations before us, the church today has embarked on a course of change in worship to reach out. When the Spirit leads, Jesus Christ will be praised and God will be worshiped. We have a biblical vision to inform us. We have priorities to guide us: faithfulness to the gospel, freedom, and love. God has provided the gifts and resources; Jesus has given us the call. It is our time to dare something in the name of Christ.

When the Spirit leads, Jesus Christ will be praised and God will be worshiped.

CHAPTER 3

Postmodern Culture and Contexts

Sally Morgenthaler

Elaine is a pastor in a Midwestern city of 80,000 people. Her congregation has a 125-year history, and she has served there for the last four years. All in all, things have gone well. In terms of church membership, there were 133 members when she came, and at last count, there were 107. She figures that is pretty good for a congregation where the average adult age is sixty-two.

As the congregation continues to shrink, though, the community is experiencing a resurgence. Considering this irony, Elaine has tried to recall any significant bends in the road. Sundays and holidays have come and gone like clockwork. Only a few patterns have changed. Funerals are on the upswing—there were seven in the last nine months. She is down to just the occasional wedding—usually for people who aren't members of the congregation.

Brides liked the church's stained-glass and carved communion rail. Additionally, the confirmation class definitely has decreased. Only four

Sally Morgenthaler, Littleton, Colorado, speaks and consults on issues of worship and postmodern culture. She is an author, photographer, and musician with a passion for creating and nurturing sacred space.

members this year, but she figures that is to be expected. It's an older congregation, after all.

Still, there are days—more this year than last—when she can't help wondering what has happened. The sanctuary was constructed in the 1920s for 300 worshipers, but more than three decades have passed since attendance has come close to reaching that capacity. She feels fortunate if there are seventy people in worship on any given Sunday.

New families move into the neighborhood each month. A significant number of them are first-generation immigrants. Each morning, Elaine enjoys watching the stylish high-schoolers gather at the bus stop just outside her office window. Other newcomers are part of an unpredicted influx of young professional couples: two-income twenty-something couples who prefer the downtown environment to the suburbs. Some of these couples have infants and toddlers, and have trouble finding good day-care options in the city.

Elaine thinks about starting a day-care center. If the truth be known, she thinks about a lot of new things she would like to do for this community. Yet, there seems to be little to no congregational interest in connecting with these "outsiders." As much as she has tried to initiate conversations on community outreach, weekly meetings bog down in purely operational issues: reports on building maintenance, minor facility updates (like adding microwave oven in the kitchen), and simply making sure the bills get paid. Elaine wonders, "Is this really all church is about?" Surely she attended seminary and answered God's call to do more than this.

Last week, a few of the "younger" members—all forty-somethings and parents of confirmands—asked Elaine if they could start a mid-week contemporary service. They wanted something with energy and spontaneity, something that connected with their kids. Not coincidentally, this group had recently attended a contemporary service at a megachurch in the suburbs. Elaine didn't think she was going to live through their one-hour-plus, effusive description.

Elaine was in a quandary. More than a few of her clergy colleagues had found themselves in severe battle mode over starting a contemporary worship service. On the other hand, she thought of her four confirmands and of the community surrounding the church. The Presbyterian congregation

The lifestyles, concerns, and spiritual orientation of the people who live around us have shifted drastically.

down the street had hired a company to do some demographic studies of the area. The upshot was that 72 percent of the people living within a three-mile radius of her church did not attend worship anywhere.

Elaine sat in her office, watching a group of teenagers gather on the sidewalk outside. Would a renovated worship style attract their families? Better still, would it attract them? Then she caught herself. "Silly idealism," she thought. "What if all that contemporary stuff was just a suburban thing? What if it only really worked in places that looked like theaters or conference facilities, in churches that could afford teal-colored, upholstered seats, automated screens, and ready-made rug art? What if it only attracted "consumer Christians"—disgruntled people from other churches, not those who had never attended church?

One thing she knew. This was a congregation that was not going to give up very easily its connection to the past. From mahogany pews to the ornate candelabra carved by the founding pastor, from the "Jesus in the Garden of Gethsemane" stained-glass window to the eternal light, this church was simply not going to adopt a silk-plant, color-coordinated outfit approach without at least a significant skirmish. If only there were more options.

Return to sender

Elaine's story—her congregation's story—is shared by many of us in North American ministry. Whether we are in urban, suburban, or rural settings, this is our common dilemma: the lifestyles, concerns, and spiritual orientation of the people who live around us have shifted drastically—so drastically, that our church no longer offers what they need to engage with God. Change has definitely not slowed so that we can catch up.

It is now the rare church where the core membership actually reflects the third-millennial character of its larger community. The features of this community are: a multiplicity of worldviews, digitalization, intense interest in spiritual matters, and the experience of brokenness. And this is the case whether our congregation's core culture is sixth-generation Western European, African-American, or baby-boomer-suburban. The reality is, most North American churches have become cultural islands in a large, confounding sea. And the tide is rising quickly.

Noted theologian Helmut Thielicke reminds us that the gospel must be repeatedly forwarded to "a new address" because the recipient is repeatedly changing places of residence. Aware of cultural isolation, many ministry leaders have dutifully followed Thielicke's advice and spent the last twenty years forwarding gospel mail. This is laudable effort, unless, of course, you happen to have an outdated forwarding address on file. If that is the case, the net result is a whole lot of wasted effort.

Here is just one example of how the lack of connection with our unchurched neighbors can trigger "return to sender" responses. In an attempt to reach out, we say we want to widen the circle of worship. Yet, most of the people we hope to gather into our sanctuaries don't see themselves in any way as being "outside the circle." They are spiritual people with spiritual journeys and enough spiritual resources at their fingertips to fill the Library of Congress. As we look to the future, it is crucial that leaders recognize the vastly altered spiritual landscape and it is quite simply, this: North Americans don't feel they need to come to church to encounter God. They have Oprah Winfrey, *Harry Potter,* and nirvana.com. They can go to the video store and rent recent supernatural films such as *The Sixth Sense, Stigmata,* and *Unbreakable.* Who needs church? It's time we find out where the people we are trying to reach really live.

> **Their question is not "Is there a God?" Their question is "Which one?"**

Address update, part 1

People today are spiritually driven and aware. Our neighbors are not atheists looking to join a Madelyn Murray O'Hair chapter. Neither are they looking for ten proofs for the resurrection. Their question is not, "Is there a God?" Their question is "Which one?" and they want a deeply personal, life-changing relationship with the God they assume is there. So, what does the church have to offer when the whole world has become a cathedral; where sacred space is whatever space you are in; where the God of the church comes across as multidimensional as a piece of cardboard and as exciting as Milquetoast; where endless denominational statements, autopilot rituals, theological hairsplitting, and religious propositions have crowded out spiritual experience. In this milieu, the church is one of the last places any self-respecting citizen of the new millennium would go to look for God. This is the real spiritual habitat of the seekers in your community, regardless of age or ethnicity.

Address update, part 2

Many people living in your community are fractured people living in an increasingly fractured world. And they know it. They have no illusions about where life on this planet is headed. For them, human progress is an oxymoron. The dream of utopia breathed its last about a decade ago. How has the church responded? Not very well, but surprisingly enough, it is the so-called contemporary church that has particularly ignored this development in the human journey. Just as the cracks of people's lives have been opening up—spilling the ooze of human depravity in unprecedented visibility—the contemporary church has continued to proffer positive thinking and steps to victorious living—essentially, human-centered strategies that are not only counter to the gospel, but embarrassingly outdated in an increasingly cynical, realistic culture. (Remember the Isaiah 64:6 reference to filthy rags?)

Perhaps you were one of the thousands of ministry leaders who visited fast-growing megachurches in the 1980s and early 1990s before cynicism became entrenched as a cross-generational, cross-racial mindset. Since that time, many new controversies and concerns have affected the nation: Rodney King, global ethnic "cleansing," the Oklahoma City bombing, the O. J. Simpson trial, DNA harvesting, cyberterrorism, cybersex, Columbine, and Jonesboro, exponential missionary killings, and a botched national election. The list goes on and on. You remember watching in amazement as tens of thousands of people filled impossibly cavernous worship centers. You marveled at these congregations' efficiency, at their passion for the irreligious. And you went back home with new hope—determined to fill what now seemed like a curiously diminutive, outdated, and ordinary sanctuary.

Questions that won't go away

There were just a few nagging problems. The first was how to reach the uninitiated in your community without sacrificing what you know to be true:

- Worship as sacred act, holy encounter; an expression of divinely initiated relationship.

- Worship as whole-person response, not limited to emotions that could be considered the subset of "happy."
- Historic Christian worship as celebration and lament, praise and repentance, thanksgiving and longing, faith and doubt, assurance and unanswered questions, clarity and mystery, imminence and transcendence.
- Your task: to take the three shining gems of the church growth era—repackaging, excellence, and passion—and apply them to the creation of sacred space, to worship. What a challenge.

Then there was the nagging question, How do glitzy and simplistic work in a "post-naïve" culture? When the "__ __ __ __ happens" bumper sticker becomes the mantra of North American life, it would seem that the church's response has to change. You thought of the unchurched couple whose apartment is next door to your mother-in-law. Julio and Melissa have lived together for nearly two years. Despite their daughter Christina's arrival, they have no plans to get married. Your mother-in-law has become close to Melissa and has shared bits and pieces of Melissa's story along the way. It seems that Melissa's dad sexually abused her and her three sisters for years before abandoning the family. An adolescence of psychological depression and food stamps left Melissa understandably wary of anything close to commitment. Besides, Christina had been born with spina bifida, and Julio would lose his health insurance if he claimed her as a dependent. On your last visit to your mother-in-law, you helped Julio move a desk into their apartment and mustered up the courage to invite them to church. Julio seemed interested, but Melissa insisted, "Thanks, but we just wouldn't fit in."

You drove home, concerned and confounded. Melissa was right. They wouldn't fit in to most of the congregations in your area. After all, those congregations were "nice" places—tidy institutions targeted to married people with two incomes, good jobs, and religious upbringings. You wondered, "Just what small group would Julio and Melissa fit into?" Was there one for people who didn't have two incomes, a nice house, an SUV, and a stock portfolio? Was there a group for people who had grown up in an era of defiant crosses and gang symbols? No, Melissa and Julio weren't candidates for "nice."

When the "__ __ __ __ happens" bumper sticker becomes the mantra, the church's response has to change.

Does God know this address?

What had happened to the world? For some reason, you couldn't get the image of the *Jurassic Park* scientists out of your head. So much for human power and ingenuity. From the *Jurassic Park* films, the most intelligent species on the planet bungles the job at every turn, leaving chaos and destruction in its not-so-godlike wake.

Remember the film *American Beauty*? No suburban charm here. No *Leave It to Beaver* nice. For two excruciating hours, you gazed at your community's addictions, at the decimation in perfect middle-class families. And then it hit you. The world you were trying to reach lay in shards, way beyond the help of the religious how-to lists and smiley-faced worship choruses you had been given as worship alternatives in the 1980s and 1990s. From your sixteen-year-old's fixation with music to your cousin's recent prison term; from the prolonged demise of "Up with People" to Julio and Melissa's plight, you came face to face with humanity's new address: the postmodern world. The world of the "not-so-nice." A world where, despite all our best efforts, "__ __ __ __ happens" and there's no government, no scientific organization, and no religious guru who can make it all better.

Worship in a postmodern culture

To the well-meaning couple in Elaine's congregation, the problem of outreach was a simple one to solve. Just start a contemporary service like the one they had attended. The people will come.

They just may. The curious, the already religious but restless, those somehow hanging on to the illusion of human goodness and control. Those people might be called *moderns*. But what of the *postmoderns*? The ones in Elaine's community? The Thai immigrant family working fifteen hours a day in order to afford a two-room apartment? Twenty-somethings on relational and addiction conveyor belts? The single mother with five children under the age of six? She doubted any of these groups of people would be drawn to what was essentially a model created for optimistic, 1980s suburbia.

Elaine's reticence to accept her parishioners' advice seemed, at the time, selfish and defensive. Yet, the reality is, Elaine's instincts were right on target. That's because Elaine has actually lived at the postmodern address for a while. She herself is on an intense spiritual journey and the baggage she carries with her is not exactly carry-on size. Let's just say, her life has been far from the Barbie-doll fairy tale of her first-grade dreams. Whether she recognizes it or not, Elaine already knows where to send the package: to people like herself, to a spiritually ravenous, deeply broken, chaotic world. All she needs now is the post office box and the zip code.

So, for Elaine and for those who despite two decades of contemporary worship models are still getting boxes back marked "Return to Sender. Address Unknown" here are some mailing guidelines. They are for creating worship services that resonate with the postmoderns living at your doorstep, whether that is the inner city, suburbia, or rapidly morphing rural America.

No blank slates

As much as you might like to start fresh, to jettison everything from your congregation's present or past order of worship might have the unfortunate result of becoming irrelevant to everyone. With front porches, sambas, and icons making a come back, the answer is not the elimination of the past, but incorporating the past with the now. So, if your traditional service starts with a call-to-worship, consider customizing a new kind of gathering experience. One congregation decided to focus on the Gospel of John over the summer. Their call-to-worship featured the following done concurrently: dancers lighting a central candle; a corporate, paraphrased reading of John 1:1-3; a projected image of an exploding nebulae; and underpinning it all, an atmospheric rendition of "Come Thou Long Expected Jesus" played by the band.

The bottom line is this: your congregation has a rich history of worship form. Use it to jump-start creative, worship-faithful responses to God.

Create experiences

Today we live in an experience culture. Regardless of age or ethnicity, visceral impact and transformation is expected. From theme malls to car stereo systems powerful enough to vibrate a city block, we want to have something happen to us. In a word, we want to be "moved."

Your congregation has a rich history of worship form.

The Bible doesn't say, "Understand and figure out that the Lord is good." It says, "O, taste and see that the LORD is good!" (Psalm 34:8). If we have any hope of widening the circle in this multisensory, interactive world, congregational leaders need to orient worship services to experiences, not head trips. This does not mean skimping on content. It simply means that the content of who God is, what God has done, and who we are as a result is delivered in the context of experience rather than as concepts.

It's time we gave people something not only to hear, but also to see, touch, taste, and smell.

It's time we gave people something not only to hear, but also to see, touch, taste, and smell. It's time to shift from services that are merely props for preaching to services that preach: visually, musically, and tangibly. When the common currency of communication has shifted from print to image, we especially need to incorporate visual art: digital and painted, sculpted and photographed, animated and sketched. Why not celebrate a six-week old infant's adoption into a family via home video? Or, for your next Christmas Eve service, try setting a solo rendition of Christina Rosetti's "In the Bleak Midwinter" to a black and white photographic collage of urban young couples. Jesus was born to a homeless couple in Bethlehem. But he could have been born in your own city, to a homeless, destitute pair living under a bridge.

The key is, expand the worship palette of the congregation. Exchange the box of eight crayons for a box of 120. From the scent of crushed juniper berries during an Advent ritual to the feel of callused fingers and oil during prayer; from silken strands of cloth—remnants representing the mantle of ministry God would pass to us—to the taste and texture of bitter herbs on Maundy Thursday, these God will use to draw us close, to make Creator, Redeemer, and Sanctifier known. Out of the realm of religion and into our realities. After all, is this not what God accomplished in Philippians 2:2-11? God who knew no form, took on form so that we might live. Our task: to re-Incarnate the Incarnate and let God again speak through the mundane, the material, the fruit of our own human clay.

Communicate via story

There are many leaders who are understandably wary of the term *experience*. But, essentially, experience simply returns people to their story, to their own life journeys. Information cannot do that. Information is about abstraction. It is no respecter of individuality, no keeper of days, no remembrance of relationship. Stories, by their very nature, are interactive and personal. They are dynamic and changing. Stories breath, inspire, and alter the course of history. Which is why there are more than thirty renditions of *Chicken Soup for the Soul* on the bookstore shelves; why going out to the movies and renting videos have become integral activities for most families; why ESPN programming is biography interspersed with sports and not vice-versa; and why Jesus told parables. Just try to find an account of the Son of God preaching a three-point sermon!

Yet, a word of caution needs to be mentioned here. A return to story is not enough. To widen the circle of Christian worship, congregational leaders must connect people's stories with *the* story. Frank Senn, author of *Christian Liturgy,* maintains that worship is "enacting God's story to a world that has lost its story." He argues, "[We] must provide what people lack: . . . a narratable world, coherent meaning, and a way of enacting it. If the world has come apart . . . the church must redo the world. It must provide an aimless present with a usable past and a hope-filled future" (Fortress Press, 1997, p. 698).

What should buoy every spirit intent upon the task of relevance—the re-Incarnation of the gospel in a new millennium—is this: at the postmodern address, there is finally room for God's story. And there is room precisely because the human story has failed. After 300 years, human beings are looking for a God outside of themselves, a God bigger than themselves. For the first time since the Enlightenment, most will admit that they are looking for a God who can enter and heal their shattered lives.

Telling the story at worship today: A father and son enact the story of the prodigal son in readers' theater style as Rembrandt's glorious etching, *The Return of the Prodigal Son*, is projected in the background. A local artist sketches the figure of Elizabeth as a ninety-year-old woman retells the story of John the Baptist's birth. As the painter continues to paint, the old woman expands the story to include her own, reminiscing about God's faithfulness and the visions divinely brought to fruition in her life and the lives of those close to her.

Recently, I attended a worship service filled with people in their twenties. Most of them had never heard the account of David and Bathsheba (2 Samuel 11), but they sat on the edge of the scratched mahogany pews in an aging, downtown church and they listened. There was no screen this

Congregational leaders must connect people's stories with the story.

time and no music. Yet, they were mesmerized as the thirty-five-year-old pastor retold the story—without notes. At the end, there was no "take-home," no three-point application. The pastor simply sat down and two people, a man and a woman, got up. They began telling their own story. They were a couple who had experienced the effects of adultery and were, in many ways, still struggling to stay together. No riding off into the sunset. No pink bows. Just the plain, God-inhabited truth.

There may be plenty of "reality" shows on TV, but the church has real-life stories of those being redeemed; those whose shattered places are encountering the Savior, and they need to be heard.

Plan worship in community

Worship needs to be planned in community if it is to reflect our God who is, first and foremost, community.

Worship that resonates with postmoderns is not business as usual. There is absolutely no way that the "lone ranger" approach to worship planning is going to suffice in this new landscape. Whether it's reconstituting the old into new configurations, planning multisensory experiences, or telling effective story—all this takes time, creativity, and resources. Ministry leaders could just stop here, close the book, and leave reaching postmoderns to the other 3,000-plus churches. We could, if it weren't for the fact that God has called us to faithfulness. And for the God-carved window of opportunity for becoming the priesthood of all believers we say that we are. Because, beyond the pragmatic reasons listed above, worship needs to be planned in community if it is to reflect our God who is, first and foremost, community: Creator, Redeemer, Sanctifier.

The first step is the most important and perhaps the most difficult. And that is, to pledge that, if it is within your power, you will never again plan another worship service all alone. Starting with the service you have yet to put on paper, invite a staff member or lay leader into the brainstorming process. It should be someone to whom you are close emotionally, spiritually, one who is known to be a private as well as public worshiper, and, preferably, a person who routinely thinks "outside the lines." Begin a weekly dialogue with your partner, perhaps over coffee or lunch. But the important thing is to begin. Don't let another week go by.

Make your meetings relational and casual, but be sure to come with a focus of theme, Scripture reading, seasonal treatment, mood, or story.

Once the ideas start flowing, it will be easy to get bogged down in an ocean of possibility, so try to limit yourself to one new kind of experience per week—even if that experience takes only sixty seconds out of the entire service.

After you and your planning partner are comfortable with each other, invite two or three more people into the process. Possible candidates: visual and digital artists, writers, musicians, technicians, and at least one "implementer." This is someone who may have little artistic ability per se, but who can see the steps a specific task will take and will not only keep restating the vision of a particular service or series, but prod those involved until the task is done.

Over time, your weekly worship planning community may become the hub of a much larger community, essentially forming an entire web of artistic, technical, and implementation communities—all interconnected by the common task of creating sacred space. A literary group might paraphrase Scripture, create indigenous creeds, or write short, poetic responses. A team of dancers could promote an entire array of movement—from mime to more stylized movement such as ballet and modern dance. An ambiance committee could concentrate simply on the week-to-week worship environment, providing variety with fabric, paintings, photos, sculpture, and candles. The technical crew—sound, light, graphics, and projection—could work closely with musicians, artists, photographers, and videographers to provide a rich digital backdrop. And finally, the musicians' community could expand from a worship team (instrumentalists and vocalists) to a community including both choral groups and "unplugged" musicians group (classical and acoustic instrumentalists).

The list could go on and the chapters that follow explore the possibilities further. The CD-ROM contains material to help you in your planning. "Attention-to-Context Checklist," CD Resource 3A, provides practical ways to explore the contextual questions raised in this chapter. What is essential is the body-of-Christ vision of artists gathered around task, their respective leaders (the hub) meeting weekly to chart out the details and trajectory of each week's venture into God-encounters. And as these communities roll up their sleeves, as they create a setting for experiences of God, they will have the incredible, unmatched opportunity to be "Jesus-with-

See CD Resource 3A

skin-on" to each other and to the unchurched artists that will be invited into their process. This is church as it was meant to be and worship planning that reflects the multihued, multitextured, communal nature of the One we adore.

Elaine's new groove

Elaine took a big step a month ago. She invited the couple—yes, the very pair that had suggested starting a new service—to be her weekly worship planning partners. When she shared some of her musings about the community, about the changes in the culture, and about her vision for experiential worship, they could not contain their excitement. They have met at the Thai restaurant down the street for two Mondays now. Lots of lemon grass soup and pud thai, but between bites and glasses of water to put out all the fire, new worship dreams are taking shape. Who knows, maybe that 300-seat worship space won't be big enough in a few years.

CHAPTER 4

Worship Patterns and Music Selection

Richard Webb

The apostle Paul was passionate about communicating the gospel. He wanted everyone to experience the love, power, and new vision for life that Christ had given him. For Paul, Jesus was everything. Nothing could stand in the way of that message. "I have become all things to all people," he wrote to the church in Corinth (1 Corinthians 9:22). Paul would do just about anything to help people experience the gospel with clarity and power. Particularly when it came to worship, Paul insisted that the gospel be proclaimed clearly. He instructed the Corinthians either to prophesy or to accompany their speaking in tongues with the gift of interpretation. That way both modes of proclamation would be effective in the ears of their hearers. "If the bugle gives an indistinct sound," he wrote, "who will get ready for battle? So with yourselves; if in a tongue you utter speech that is not intelligible, how will anyone know what is being said?" (1 Corinthians 14:8-9). Paul believed the stakes were high. If in worship the hearer could not understand what was being proclaimed the consequences could be eternally disastrous.

The issue of clarity and intelligibility in worship concerns not just the spoken word; it encompasses the whole of worship experience. This chapter

---

Richard Webb is teaching pastor at Lutheran Church of Hope, West Des Moines, Iowa, where he serves as coordinator of worship life.

explores how effectively planned worship patterns, and the music within those patterns, can help pave the way for worshipers to experience God's power, truth, and grace. But first, here is a brief review of recent history.

Ritual patterns, a history

Worship planning is more than a fill-in-the-blanks exercise.

As recent at thirty years ago, Christians in North American used essentially two patterns in their worship: the Mass and the Prone. Used predominantly within Roman Catholic, Orthodox, Lutheran, and Anglican circles, the traditional Mass was often understood by both insiders and outsiders as a complex sequence of chants, litanies, scripted prayers, and prescribed biblical readings. Music written for the Mass, both old and new, adhered to old traditions based on either Roman and Anglican Chant or the Reformation Chorale. At its best, the Mass and its music invoked in worshipers a profound sense of mystery and awe. However, its elaborate ritual structure could also become difficult to follow, both for the newcomer as well as the initiated.

Initially a fairly simple ritual, the Prone was adopted by Reformed and Free Church groups in reaction to the perceived formalism and complexity of the traditional Mass. Particularly in North America, this worship form and its music reflected the informal style of southern rural and working class culture. However, over time both its ritual structure and music also increased in complexity. Like the Mass, it ran the danger of becoming difficult for the worshiper to comprehend.

In the 1960s, the problem of intelligibility in worship had become so acute that congregational leaders and liturgical scholars of all denominations began experimenting with new ways of doing and thinking about worship. As scholars in particular began focusing on the essential form of worship rather than on its details, they discovered that both the Prone and the Mass followed a basic pattern established in the second century: Gathering, Word, and Sending. In denominations that emphasized the role of the Lord's Supper the pattern was extended to include Communion and was thus: Gathering, Word, Meal, and Sending. This emphasis on the pattern of worship activity over its component parts helped leaders see worship planning as more than a fill-in-the-blanks exercise. Worship leaders began to look at their services in terms of overall flow and coherence.

Moreover, they became concerned with how worshipers were affected by what they were experiencing.

At the same time, non-Northern European ethnic groups such as African-Americans and Hispanic peoples began to assert their values and traditions into the public square. This had profound impact upon the arts, particularly within popular music. What happened in secular culture also happened in the churches. In the realm of worship, this infusion of new cultural expression was accelerated by the emerging openness of congregations toward experimentation and change. In the Roman Catholic Church, for example, liturgical music from immigrant Hispanic culture became well-known within predominantly European-American parishes. Within the Protestant community, traditional suburban congregations began to draw heavily upon African-American gospel music and Appalachian folk music for their singing. Composers of almost every Christian tradition, European and non-European alike, began to experiment with popular music styles as a source for new worship music. As a result, the array of choices for congregational singing increased exponentially.

Another important driver for change in worship was the spiritual and worship renewal movements that swept across many denominations in the 1970s and 1980s. In the traditionally white denominations, these renewal movements led many congregations to rediscover the affective nature of worship. These congregations then began to move toward a simplified and more visceral expression of Gathering, Word, and Sending. Within their services they often included a Gathering time that contained up to forty-five minutes of praise, adoration, and confession through songs and choruses written in popular style. This portion of the service was often referred to as "Praise and Worship." As the church growth movement spread throughout North America in the 1980s, other more traditional congregations adopted the Praise and Worship style of gathering as a way of helping unchurched people, who often had no exposure to traditional church music, feel more at home in their services. This strategy also worked extremely well with suburban baby boomers, whose culture was responsible for producing many of the musical styles used in these new services.

This strategy, however, did not always work well with their children. Beginning in the mid-1980s, significant shifts in the way people thought about life and made sense of experience brought about major changes in

Renewal movements led many congregations to rediscover the affective nature of worship.

North American popular culture. These changes also produced a significant cultural gap between the relatively homogeneous Boomers, who had
already participated in one major cultural shift, and the diversity-savvy
generations that came after them. Responding to these shifts, congregations dedicated to reaching these younger generations once again began
experimenting with worship patterns. But this time they headed in
altogether new directions through the use of *bricollage.*

A bricollage is an assemblage of diverse and contrasting elements placed together into a new, useful, and coherent form.

Already present in popular media culture, such as music videos and the
Internet, a bricollage is an assemblage of diverse and contrasting elements
placed together into a new, useful, and coherent form. In terms of worship
pattern, that means worshipers might experience in one service such
wildly diverse elements as incense, demonstrative worship expression,
ancient litanies and creeds, Byzantine icons, Microsoft® PowerPoint®
presentations, and short clips from contemporary films. For musicians,
bricollage often means combining into one service such diverse styles as
Gregorian chant, Seattle grunge, Latin American salsa, and South African
pop. This is not an attempt at so-called "blended" worship—a compromise
strategy aimed at lowering the tension between existing cultural and generational groups attending the same service. Rather, worship as a bricollage
is the evolution of a new form, one coherent with the language of the
emerging diverse North American postmodern culture. So, where do we go
from here?

- How do we plan for worship within a constantly evolving cultural
  situation—where familiar descriptions like "traditional" and "contemporary" are rendered utterly meaningless, where generalized worship
  "solutions," which may have worked in the past, are now profoundly
  unhelpful?
- How do worship leaders respond faithfully this situation of rapid
  change and radical diversity?

Building on the essential patterns

As noted previously, the basic form of Christian corporate worship con-
sists of four building blocks: Gathering, Word, Meal, and Sending. While
the overall pattern of worship is relatively simple, the range of possibilities
inside each component is wide. Since some possibilities will work better

than others, we need to determine what works most faithfully for our particular situation. Below is a brief survey of the function of each building block, how they relate to other building blocks, and how they are influenced by the context. It's important to remember that in worship these building blocks do not necessarily need to follow the order in which they are listed below. More important is how they relate to each other and the effect they have upon the worshiper.

Gathering

In the Gathering portion of the service, worshipers spend time opening themselves up to God's presence. In services where the Lord's Supper is celebrated, this actually happens twice, once before the proclamation of the Word and again before worshipers feast at the Lord's table. Historically, worshipers have prepared themselves to experience God's presence in many ways: invitation, witness and proclamation, praise, meditation, confession of sin, prayer for others, and prayers for openness, to name a few. In some congregations, gathering patterns are very elaborate; in others, they are very simple.

Four essential building blocks: Gathering, Word, Meal, and Sending.

Congregations reaching out to unchurched adults often employ the Praise-and-Worship style of Gathering. These ways of Gathering can happen before the Word and before the Meal. Interestingly enough, this seamless activity often has all the components of more elaborate and traditional gathering patterns. For example, a time of Praise and Worship might begin with "Come, Now Is the Time to Worship" (Brian Doerksen, Vineyard) functioning as the call to worship, followed by an informal spoken welcome. "I See the Lord" (Paul Baloche, Integrity) and "Thank You for Saving Me" (Martin Smith, Curious? Music) might function as hymns of praise and adoration. Afterward, "Be Magnified" (Lynn DeShazo, Integrity) might be sung as a confession, followed by "He Is Faithful" (John Barnett, Vineyard) as a proclamation of the forgiveness God offers us.

By contrast, Gathering patterns in congregations serving postmodern culture are often quite short. Mars Hill Fellowship, a Seattle congregation reaching effectively into postmodern culture, organizes their Gathering ritual in this way. They often begin their worship in silence and near darkness. A reader may break the silence by reading a psalm of lament followed by a slow and melancholy congregational song of confession such as

"Prayer" (Paul Mossburger, Deep Heaven Music). The Gathering may conclude with an assurance of forgiveness or an informal prayer or both. An extended period of praise may also be part of the service but functions more as a response to the message or the Lord's Supper than as a preparation for God's word.

- How will your congregation prepare to hear the Word?
- How will they gather around God's word, both in proclamation and in the Lord's Supper, in such a way that both member and guest alike receive message of God's truth with clarity and power?

Word

God desires to plant the Living Word firmly into the heart and minds of all worshipers. So how do we communicate this saving Word deeply into the lives of those gathered for worship? Obviously one of the primary ways is with the message or sermon. In fact, preaching is so important that an entire chapter is devoted to this subject. (See chapter 6, "Preaching That Reaches Members and Guests.") But there are other powerful ways to "preach it" as well. Particularly in a postliterate, multicultural, Internet-driven culture, where people learn through a multitude of simultaneous and diverse venues, worship leaders are challenged to consider how all aspects of the worship experience—ritual, music, media, environment—proclaim the Word.

That means that sometimes a drama might be paired with the sermon in proclaiming God's word. In some cases a drama might take place inside the sermon in order to bring home a difficult or painful point with some humor. Another way to leverage the communication of God's word might be with a vocal or instrumental solo, or an interpretive dance. At other times a reading done in a creative manner before, during, or after the message can help deepen the receptivity of the worshiper to the proclamation of the word. Silence at strategic places can also be helpful. Other moves can be equally effective. Ecclesia, a congregation in Houston that reaches out to the local artists' community, uses interpretive visual art such as sculpting or painting as a way to open up the message. Sometimes this art is created during the message, thus making available multiple and simultaneous learning venues to the worshiper. Ginghamsburg United Methodist

A reading done in a creative manner before, during, or after the message can help deepen the receptivity of the worshiper.

Church outside of Dayton, Ohio, makes extensive use of film and multimedia both to prepare and reinforce the message.

- What might be ways your congregation can creatively proclaim God's word?
- Given the cultural language of your local community, what might help pave the way in your context for the coming of the Lord?

Meal

In the last ten years congregations of all denominations have rediscovered the healing and transforming presence of Christ at the Lord's table. Local churches in all kinds of settings are exploring creative ways to help worshipers experience God's amazing grace in terms of both worship pattern and music. What does that look like? To begin with, the early church celebrated the Lord's Supper as a separate service. For that reason, the Lord's Supper shares at least two of the essential building blocks of any Christian worship service, Gathering and Word.

Gathering: Three chief ways Christian believers become open to God's presence are by naming the truth about ourselves in confession, singing songs of praise and thanksgiving, and praying for a deeper awareness of God's presence. When these are done as preparation for the Lord's Supper, they are often focused around the themes of Isaiah's great vision (Isaiah 6:1-8).

- God made known in power and presence.
- God made known in truth that exposes sin and brokenness.
- God made known in grace, forgiveness, and reconciliation.
- God calling worshipers to live lives of proclamation.

These four themes can be expressed in any number of ways: through an extended time of informal singing, a period of guided meditation accompanied by instrumental music, informal prayers of thanksgiving recalling God's saving acts in history, even a time of self-examination and confession. The level of formality would vary according to the context. In cultural contexts that rely on print for information and learning, scripted prayers and dialogues for both leaders and congregation might serve as the basis for gathering around the Lord's table. In settings where more interactive venues such as the Internet are the primary sources of learning, prayers might be spontaneous and the entire gathering strategy multimedia in scope.

Word: The greatest gift of the Lord's Supper is that worshipers not only hear but actually feast on God's living Word for them. It is here at the Lord's table that worshipers most deeply experience the intimate friendship, forgiveness, and healing of the One who gave his life for us. If only for this reason, worship leaders are called to do their utmost to help worshipers become aware of God's presence for them. In the Lord's Supper the *doing* of the Word occurs in two ways: the proclamation of the Words of Institution and the distribution of the bread and the cup. At Faith Lutheran Church in Lake Forest, Illinois, the presider proclaims the Words of Institution through an informal narrative of the Lord's Supper. On occasion he or she even combines themes from the sermon into the narrative as well. This helps the congregation focus on the particular ways Christ's presence in the meal works forgiveness and healing. At the conclusion of the narrative the presider invites the congregation to pray the Lord's Prayer as a way of naming the kingdom relationship they have through Christ at his table.

A unique hospitality challenge for congregations who have large numbers of unchurched guests in their worship services is what to do at the time of the Lord's Supper. How are we to be faithful to the biblical intent of the Supper yet extend hospitality to our guests? Some congregations have experimented with Martin Luther's strategy—which he set forth in the *Deutsche Messe* (*Luther's Works,* vol. 53, pp. 78-80)—of providing an explanation of what happens at the meal and what that means for the participants. Sometimes this explanation occurs before the Words of Institution. At other times the explanation takes the form of an invitation before the distribution of the Supper. Here the leader explains the Supper and then invites all who desire the lordship, forgiveness, and new life Christ offers to come forward and receive these promises in the bread and cup. This move is similar to a traditional altar call, only worshipers are invited not to make a decision for Christ, rather to receive Christ's decision for them.

- How might you as a worship leader help your congregation more deeply experience Christ's healing and forgiving presence in the Lord's Supper?

• How will members and guests alike be invited to experience with power and clarity Christ's life-giving decision for them?

Sending

In the early church, at the conclusion of the Lord's Supper, worshipers gave away food and money to be taken after the service to those in need. For them the connection was clear. God's new life was not only given *to* God's people, it was given *through* God's people as well. As the prophet Isaiah discovered, it is almost impossible to experience God without being moved toward some kind of response (Isaiah 6). Here are some ways congregations have sought to express this connection.

Many congregations in the Evangelical tradition conclude their services in an intentionally "unfinished" manner by dismissing the congregation almost immediately after the sermon. This way the congregation is called to continue their act of "spiritual worship" (Romans 12:1) through the active practice of faith in their daily lives.

Congregations reaching out to people within postmodern culture often spend fifteen to thirty minutes after the sermon or Lord's Supper singing everything from reflective songs of commitment and gratitude to high-energy songs of praise, proclamation, and thanksgiving. This helps bring home the magnitude of the gift Jesus has given them.

Another way many congregations bridge the gap between experience and response is to give worshipers homework assignments, such as a daily spiritual exercise that helps worshipers live in God's way for them.

• What are some ways of helping your congregation respond intentionally to the experience of God's presence?
• What would help worshipers walk with such power and confidence in the world that others would see Jesus through them?

Review and use "Worship Planning Guide" on the CD-ROM, which is designed to help you evaluate and make decisions about your worship patterns.

It is almost impossible to experience God without being moved toward some response.

See CD Resource 4A

Choosing the right music

Planning worship services with care and sensitivity is extremely important. The flow of the worship pattern must be intelligible to member and guest alike. But planning the pattern is only half the job. Choosing the right music is just as crucial. Music for worship must speak God's truth and grace with the same power and clarity as the flow of the worship pattern. Here are some things to consider in choosing music for worship.

What makes a melody?

Music for worship must speak God's truth and grace with power and clarity.

Basic to any congregational song is an effective melody. When selecting music for congregational singing, keep in mind these factors.

The melody is easy to learn without sheet music. Because fewer people today read music, it's important that worshipers are able to sing the melody with confidence after hearing it a second time. That also means that the music team must present the melody as clearly as possible.

The melody is easy to remember. Writers of popular music are well aware that any top forty song must be memorable to the hearers. The same is true for congregational music. If the melody is easy to retain it will be easier to learn.

The melody is interesting and engaging. Regardless of the ease or difficulty of the melody, it must be interesting and engaging to the worshiper. Otherwise, why bother learning it? In fact the more engaging a given melody, the more difficult it can be to learn. There are numerous songs for worship that are difficult yet extremely popular. The praise song "All Things Are Possible" (Darlene Zschech) and the hymn "Lift High the Cross" (Sydney H. Nicholson) are just two such examples. An interesting melody increases the worshiper's focus and motivation to learn it.

The melody is durable. Very simply put, can this song be used in worship more than three times without boring the worshiper? Durability is important. If the music lacks staying power it's usefulness in worship is greatly reduced.

Melody with text

Evaluating the melody alone is not enough. What the text expresses is just as important as the feelings the music conveys. Here are some basic criteria for choosing any kind of music accompanied by text.

The music and the text tell the truth. One of the primary functions of worship is to reveal God's truth in the face of the world's illusions. In Psalm 73, the psalmist articulates the incredible struggle God's people face when confronted with inexplicable evil: "My feet had almost stumbled; my steps had nearly slipped. For I was envious of the arrogant; I saw the prosperity of the wicked" (Psalm 73:2b-3). But everything changes when the psalmist enters God's house of worship: "When I thought how to understand this, it seemed to me a wearisome task, until I went into the sanctuary of God" (verses 16-17a). The stakes are high.

- Do the music and the texts we choose for worship tell the truth?
- Do they tell God's story or some other story?
- Do the songs worshipers sing and listen to point to Christ alone or do they imply some other source of life?

The music and the text fit together. As the array of choices for worship music increases exponentially, the question of "fit" becomes increasingly important. When choosing a particular song for worship, does the music match the weight and tone of the text? At first glance this seems like an easy criterion to apply. But is it really?

For example, the tune that accompanies "As Pants the Hart" (tune, Hugh Wilson), a hymn paraphrase of Psalm 42, conveys to most North Americans a simple and happy mood. Yet stanza three speaks of unending devastation that "falls splashing down, till round my soul a rising sea is spread" (text, Nahum Tate and Nicholas Brady). From all appearances this stanza hardly fits with the melody!

Similarly, there are a host of praise choruses whose texts speak of the incredible majesty and power of God, but whose melodies seem to sound more like jingles for a fast-food chain. In both cases, the mismatches seem obvious. But what happens when we began to take into account the cultural settings out of which these songs originated? Both examples cited above have melodies that come from cultures where the major key does not always indicate happiness. This is also the case with much of the music that comes from New Orleans. Visitors are often puzzled by the seemingly flippant Dixieland music they hear at funerals in that city. It is really flippant? Of course not. Dixieland music is that community's soul-music. That means that questions of musical and textual "fit" are ultimately contextual.

One of the primary functions of worship is to reveal God's truth in the face of the world's illusions.

They cannot be answered in the abstract. Finally worship leaders can only ask themselves if this particular tune and text fit and work within their particular context.

**What
energizes
one group
will wear
out another.**

The music and text match the context in which they will be used. As indicated above, issues of context are crucial for making good decisions about worship music. To communicate the story of God in an effective manner, we need to take seriously the cultural "languages" of those God has called us to serve. That's why chapter 3 of this book addresses the need to discern and learn the texture of the cultures in which the congregation finds itself. Here are several factors to be aware of when discerning the cultural languages of those you are serving.

First, is the culture of those God has called you to serve emotionally expressive or reserved? This question helps keep us from rushing to judgment about how people respond in the worship experience. All too often worshipers and worship services are judged as "shallow and emotional" or "cold and empty" when in fact what is observed are culturally appropriate modes of expression. This greatly affects the way music for congregational singing is chosen. What energizes one group will wear out another. What stirs one group will offend another. What comforts one group will bore another.

Second, how does the surrounding culture practice ritual in its public gatherings? This is especially helpful in planning Gathering, Communion, and Sending music strategies that connect well with those outside the church. At sports events, for example, North Americans become quite boisterous as they cheer for their team. At rock concerts, audiences participate in the performance almost as much as do the musicians on stage. North Americans get excited and involved at public gatherings. It should come as no surprise that unchurched guests often wonder at the lack of similar energy and participation in Christian worship services.

The music and text match the position in which they are used in the service. This question is crucial. In the Gathering, Meal, and Sending portions of the service, most music designed to reach seekers and younger generations is affective in nature. It's designed to feed the heart, to create openness and community between God and the worshipers. By contrast, most music used in the Word portion of the service is designed to instruct or to inspire commitment. It's more cognitive in nature. When affective music is used during this portion of the service the effect is often sentimental or shallow. Likewise, when predominately cognitive music is used in other parts of the service, the effect is often a lack of energy and ultimately boredom.

Discovering the musical language of your context

Up to this point the basic principles for choosing music for worship have been examined. Attention to musical styles is also critical. Just as the spoken word must be in the language of those God has called you to serve, so it is for musical styles. They must also match the cultural language of those you serve. So how do you choose the styles that fit your context? The categories of "traditional" and "contemporary" no longer make any sense; the field of play has grown more complex. So what has replaced those categories? Below are just a few examples of what you are likely to encounter as you work to discover the musical styles that fit your situation.

- traditional European and American hymns
- traditional and new country
- African-American gospel and praise
- white southern gospel and praise
- rap, hip-hop, and urban youth music
- rhythm and blues and traditional blues
- traditional and progressive jazz
- rock and roll
- easy-listening pop
- alternative rock
- North American folk music
- world music

The array of choices is bewildering. How do worship leaders sort out what works best for their situation? Consider the following ideas that can help you discover the musical languages of your neighborhood.

Visit record stores in your community. Ask the clerks to show you the most popular selling music CDs. Be sure also to ask who is buying them. This will help you sort out the diversity of tastes in your community.

Church consultant Bill Easum suggests you survey your city's music radio stations to find out which ones charge the most money for commercials. Most likely these stations are the most popular as well. Ask the three stations with the most expensive ads who their target audiences are and which styles these audiences prefer.

Congregational and door-to-door surveys also help you gather information. Ask people to rank their two most favorite music stations and to name the musical styles these stations play.

Bear in mind that not every worshiper will want to hear in worship the same style of music they listen to in the car. Therefore, survey worshipers regularly as to whether the music chosen has helped them experience God's presence. If not, ask them what would. Try to find out (discretely) the approximate age of those surveyed, whether they are members or guests.

Visit local coffee houses and bookstores that offer regular music events. Find out from the management who attends these events. See "Discovering the Musical Language of Your Contest," CD Resource 4C.

Where to find the right music

After you've discovered the musical styles that connect to those whom you serve, where will you find worship music composed in those styles? Below are some places to look. Use the CD Resource 4B, "Checklist for Choosing Congregational Music," to evaluate the music.

Publishing houses

There are seven major publishers that produce the bulk of new music being written for worship. Many of them offer new music subscription series in both audio and sheet music forms.

Augsburg Fortress
P.O. Box 1209
Minneapolis, MN 55440
800-328-4648
www.augsburgfortress.org
(traditional, folk, soft pop, gospel, Hispanic)

E.M.I. Christian Music Publishing
P.O. Box 5085
Brentwood, TN 37024
www.worshiptogether.com
(alternative rock, folk, British rock, Celtic)

G.I.A. Publications
7404 S. Mason Ave.
Chicago, IL 60638
www.giamusic.com
(folk, traditional, soft pop, Celtic, Hispanic)

Integrity Music
P.O. Box 851622
Mobile, AL 36685
www.integritymusic.com
(pop, country, gospel, rock, folk)

Maranatha! Music
P.O. Box 31050
Laguna Hills, CA 92654
(pop, rock and roll, gospel, rhythm and blues, country)

O.C.P. Publications
5536 N.E. Hassalo
Portland, OR 97213
(folk, traditional, soft pop, Celtic, gospel, Hispanic)

Vineyard Music Group
P.O. Box 68025
Anaheim, CA 92817
www.vineyardmusic.com
(rock, folk, gospel, alternative, rock, Celtic)

Not every worshiper will want to hear in worship the same style of music they listen to in the car.

Congregations writing their own music

Many congregations, particularly the ones reaching out to the post-modern community, are composing new music for worship. Here are two congregations known for high quality worship music.

Mars Hill Fellowship
7758 Earl Ave. N.W.
Seattle, WA 98117
www.marshill.fm
(alternative, rock, world music)

University Baptist Church
1701 Dutton St.
Waco, TX 76706
www.ubcwaco.org
(alternative, new country, Celtic)

Using secular music

Including secular music is great way to articulate a question or point of pain common to the community God has called you to reach. Often this kind of music is played or sung before the sermon that addresses the issues raised by the music. Another strategy is to slightly alter the original text so that, even though the melody and much of the text are familiar to the worshipers, the music now points in a new direction, usually toward the cross.

Copyright issues

Whatever kind of music you choose, it is important that you observe all applicable copyright laws. Mainline and Catholic publishers, such as Augsburg Fortress and G.I.A., have affordable licensing arrangements. Almost all other music publishers have licensing arrangements with C.C.L.I., a licensing service located at this address:

Christian Copyright Licensing International
17201 N.E. Sacramento St.
Portland, OR 97230
www.ccli.com

Open windows

As worship leaders our ultimate goal is that worshipers experience God's life-changing power and grace in their lives. As we plan for worship that makes this possible, we need to remember that God wants this for us as well; that we too are called to be among those who worship in spirit and in truth. Even so, it is easy for us to be so preoccupied with the logistics of worship leadership that we miss the very thing we desire for others. We know we are called to be worship leaders, but do we also know we are called as well to be "lead worshipers"? When we plan for worship, do we also worship through our planning? Do we pray constantly throughout our work and encourage others to do the same? Do we follow God's Spirit even as we lead others in worship?

As we become attentive to God's presence and leading throughout our ministry, we pave the way not only for God to bless us but also to bless others through us. And then we become what God intends for us to be: open windows of God's grace and truth, widening the circle for member and guest alike.

CHAPTER 5

Incorporating the Arts in Worship

Kathi Graves

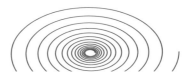

In 1974, I was a fifteen-year-old fundamentalist Baptist teenager. My church viewed pop music and school dances as sinful, and we were discouraged from listening to or taking part. Girls couldn't wear pants to church functions and co-ed swimming at church camp was taboo. The fact was, I really liked the music I heard on the radio, the dress code didn't make sense to me, and I loved to hang out at the pool during the summer with my neighborhood friends, male and female. And I also happened to love Jesus with all my heart.

Lisa and I had been friends and neighbors for five years. She wore her bell-bottom, hip-hugger jeans without hesitation. On any given day you could find her sewing or fashioning macramé jewelry in her room as she listened to the tunes of her favorite pop artists, Jackson Browne or "Sweet Baby James" Taylor. We spent countless hours together during those years. Our creative bent brought us together and provided a foundation for our friendship.

At the same time, we were very different. Through my faith in Christ, I modeled a life of joy that she knew she didn't possess during what were

---

Kathi Graves leads worship and serves as den mother to the young men in the band at Warehouse 242, a Charlotte, North Carolina, church that reaches postmoderns.

some very tumultuous adolescent years for her. I was privy to her pain and longed for my friend to know Jesus the way I knew him. If only there was a place I could take her to hear about Jesus—a place that was cool and down to earth, not irrelevant and weird; a place where she would be welcomed and not scorned; a place where she could be accepted for who she was and where her artistic talents could flourish.

Sadly, my congregation, like many of that time, was not that place. We were urged to fulfill the Great Commission, but the idea that the message of the gospel should be made relevant to people in our very community who existed outside of the church was not a typical application. Mission to non-Christians was understood as an activity that took place far away.

Today, many people in the church not only recognize our mission opportunities at home. But they have set out to accomplish that mission in much different ways, ones that perhaps more effectively represent God's desire to shine light into our darkness. Many congregations that are effectively reaching new people today are employing the arts in worship in new and renewed ways.

In *The Sacred Romance,* Brent Curtis and John Eldredge write, "Our acts of remembering [God's gracious acts] must . . . involve both essential truths and dramatic narrative. . . . We need to hold the creeds in one hand and our favorite forms of art in the other. There are films, books, poems, songs, and paintings I return to again and again for some deep reason in my heart. Taking a closer look, I see that they all tell me about some part of the Sacred Romance. They help wake me to a deeper remembrance. As Don Hudson has said, 'Art is, in the final analysis, a window on heaven'" (*The Sacred Romance,* Thomas Nelson, 1997, p. 204).

If God speaks through anything and everything, and everything is either a tool (a *means* to worship God) or an idol (a *thing* we worship), then the church's challenge is to be a place where works of art are transformed into tools of worship. The created work isn't something in itself to be worshiped, but instead, a convincing and resplendent reflection of a creative God who made us with this desire for the beautiful and a proclivity for creating beautiful things and experiences. How can we think that there's no place for the arts in worship? We seem to have defined some arbitrary line between the sacred and the secular, leaving much of what could be used as a glorious and powerful tool in the hands of someone else.

God made us with this desire for the beautiful and a proclivity for creating beautiful things.

In a recent interview with Leadership Network, senior pastor Ron Martoia of Westwinds Community Church in Jackson, Michigan, described the congregation's creative use of art: "On one hand the introduction of art into worship is obviously a very ancient thing. . . . Yet, . . . the reintroduction of art seems to be fresh and new, and somehow vibrant and different. We have been very intentional about it. It has allowed people to explore their faith in the context of ambiguity . . . that verbal communication does not. So we've been very careful to try to create some of those types of experiences. . . . It is up to us to steward those moments because it might be in a transition that somebody hears God's voice" (*Explorer: Field Notes for the Emerging Church,* no. 25, Dec 4, 2000, *Leadership Network* electronic journal).

Many art forms can easily be used in a worship setting. The rest of this chapter explores specific possibilities of how some of those art forms are being used in various congregations in order to inspire and empower you to do the same wherever you are.

Performance music

In this chapter, the term "performance music" refers to any song presented during the worship service in which the congregation does not participate. It's important to acknowledge that the term may be suspect to long-time churchgoers who have been taught that singing and playing instruments are sacred acts of worship to the Lord, *not* performances. Yet the term helps to distinguish different types of musical offerings.

Performance music is a highly effective way to proclaim God's word or to reinforce the message of the sermon. A song can illustrate a point in a way that words alone may not accomplish. Contextualization, of course, is key here. If the people you are trying to reach are primarily baby boomers, then the style of music you select will differ significantly from the music you would choose for postmoderns (the generation born between 1964 and 1981, and others who share characteristics shaped by postmodern thinking and culture).

Pop music, country music, jazz, swing, are all styles that are familiar to the general population and speak well to boomers across the board. Contemporary Christian music artists span a wide range of styles so you have vast resources from which to choose at Christian music stores or their

Web site. A live band is great but may not be realistic if you are just starting to move toward a more contemporary style. Accompaniment tapes are an easy way to get started if you lack a band that can "recreate" a musical selection with excellence. Integrity Music produces CDs that can be played from a laptop computer that is plugged directly into the sound system. They includes lyrics ready for Microsoft ® PowerPoint ® projection. Again, there are many selections available if you decide to go this route.

Live music is certainly a better choice, however, for ministry with post-moderns. Even if it must be done simply, the authenticity or "realness" of a live performance is without question more appealing to this group. Excellence is still a high value, but a raw, rough-edged performance is pre-ferred over something that is too "slick." Musical styles can vary from alternative rock to folk to techno/modern, hip-hop, world music, and even ancient hymns and chants.

At Warehouse 242, a ministry to postmoderns in Charlotte, North Carolina, performance music often is used to pose a question or present the problem, rather than reinforce the solution. The solution comes in the sermon. Therefore, popular-rock and alternative-rock songs that illustrate a greater awareness, perhaps, of the brokenness of the world are good choices because they are familiar songs to people who are outside the church. After weaving it into a new and completely different context, it can give a whole new meaning to the song.

If you are involved in cross-cultural ministry, by all means use indige-nous music forms. There is a plethora of modern music that draws from many ethnic traditions and even creates rather unlikely combinations, such as African and Celtic music, to make beautiful and interesting new sound experiences.

A raw, rough-edged performance is preferred over some-thing that is too "slick."

Drama

Many congregations that have successfully reached baby boomers have developed an approach that tends to work well across the board. "Real life" scenarios are presented as part of the worship service and depict situations illustrating common life experiences. The presentation varies from gut-wrenching emotional exchanges to slapstick comedy. It gets the point across very effectively and can be very entertaining at the same time.

Community Church of Joy in Phoenix, Arizona; Willow Creek Community Church in South Barrington, Illinois; and Forest Hill Church in Charlotte, North Carolina, all use drama extensively in their services, with quality that is nothing short of professional. One very creative example is Forest Hill's annual "winter solstice," which takes Charles Dickens's *A Christmas Carol* and fast-forwards ahead one year in the life of Ebenezer Scrooge, to the next holiday season. In this expertly crafted, immersion theater, the audience becomes house guests of Scrooge and experiences firsthand the effects of his transformation as they are served a delicious dinner and participate in the performance. Great attention is paid to the details, from the authentic costuming and décor, to the groups of carolers who meander about on the sidewalks outside the theater before and after the performance, as guests are arriving. For every ticket a congregation member purchases, they must buy another ticket for a friend who does not attend church.

Such a performance is too lofty for many of congregations, requiring resources many do not possess. But don't despair! There are so many other simple and creative ways to introduce these dramatic elements into your service For example, a monologue is easy to perform and produce and can be done in the simplest of settings. If you have someone on your team who can write original pieces, so much the better. There is good existing material available that covers just about any and every subject imaginable. See page 108 of the Resource List.

A poem that reinforces the message of the sermon can also be a very powerful element. Original poetry written by congregational participants or leaders has the advantage of relational value, so highly regarded among postmoderns, and carries with it an organic quality, representing the "voice" of that specific community.

Dance

Dance is a beautiful art form that, unfortunately, is not as widely accepted in some pockets of U.S. society, especially where fundamentalist or pietistic traditions are strong. Further, dance done poorly is a painful experience to watch. Therefore, it can be a challenge for congregations to use dance effectively, especially for the purpose of outreach.

So, how is dance best used to glorify God? If there are dancers in your community who are called to use their talents, by all means explore the possibilities. Sally Morgenthaler, the writer of chapter 3, "Postmodern Culture and Context," and the author of *Worship Evangelism* (Zondervan, 1995), has described how movement was introduced by two members who are professional dancers at the congregation where she is a member. Brief synchronized, rhythmic movement is used as a means to ease the congregation into dance as part of worship. They have started with something very simple and basic, such as two participants processing rhythmically down the center aisle to music. This simple art form can set the tone for the entire worship service.

If your outreach opportunities include particular ethnic populations, do not overlook ethnic-specific dance forms as part of worshipful expression. Done with authenticity and care, this can be a very interesting and creative way to build bridges.

Look to our roots in Jewish worship tradition. There are Jewish folk dances specific to rites of worship such as candle-lighting. Worship practices from other cultures and faith traditions can also suggest patterns of movement to incorporate in Christian worship.

Do not overlook ethnic-specific dance forms as part of worshipful expression.

Film and video

We are a society of movie-goers and TV-watchers, so why not take use them for something beyond the purpose of pure entertainment? Technology has made it easy for us to bring the medium of film and video into the church. Consult the Motion Picture Licensing Corporation about its licensing program covering the use of the videos in school, church, or other public settings (phone: 1-800-462-8835; Web site: www.mplc.com).

You can select a clip to serve the same purposes described earlier for performance music and drama. The scene you select is critical and several things must be taken into consideration in that process:

- Not everyone has seen the entire movie or program. The clip must make sense independent of the whole story.
- The clip must be strategically placed at a point in the service where it will have the most impact.

- The clip cannot be too long. People will lose interest after about five to seven minutes.
- Additionally, the person running the equipment must know exactly where to start and stop the video. Don't do it without a run-through. There is nothing more annoying or distracting than having to wait thirty seconds for the clip to begin or having no sound for the first thirty seconds.

A riveting video clip can employ images that would be difficult to equal with words alone.

A riveting video clip can visually widen the circle to all types of unchurched people by employing images that would be difficult to equal with words alone. Here is a powerful example of how a particular film clip was used to illustrate that our salvation is by grace alone and not by anything we do. In this instance, the speaker gave a brief setup: "We often attempt to earn acceptance from God and people by doing good works ourselves. To make the point that we are saved by God's grace alone, we are going to take a look at a clip from *The Mission*. The setting is in a Portuguese colonial holding in South America. Robert De Niro's character is a former slave trader, a mercenary, and a man that has murdered his brother. He sets off with the help of a priest to do a penance, a work that is intended to somehow show sorrow for sins and in some way make broken things whole again. His penance is to pull all of his armor and weapons behind him through the jungles of what today is southern Brazil and ultimately carry them up the face of a dangerous waterfall. Once at the top of the falls, he will encounter South Americans, the same people whom he has tormented, captured, and enslaved in the past."

Then the clip was shown, which culminates in a dangerous ascent up the falls and ultimately in a face-to-face confrontation with the Native Americans. At the top of the falls, still tied to armor and weapons—really his old sin and works—he is no freer after the penance than he was before it. But by an act of incredible forgiveness by his victims, De Niro's character is freed from his bondage and given life! It is a breathtaking clip.

At the end, the speaker needed only to walk back to the stage and say, "That is what God did for us. God really does forgive in extravagant ways. He frees us from our works and our sins."

Microsoft ® PowerPoint ®

More technological media options are inevitable, so if you can afford it, the investment in a system to run Microsoft PowerPoint (projector, laptop computer, screen) is well worth the money. Projecting the words to worship music, performance music, outlines of the sermon, and so forth enables us to keep our noses out of worship folders and hymnals, providing a more "inclusive" atmosphere where everyone is looking up.

Community Church of Joy in Phoenix, Arizona, utilizes an elaborate setup, consisting of two screens actually built into the wall, each facing a different section of seats so everyone can easily see a screen. Much effort goes into creating the individual slides for PowerPoint, including interesting effects, background colors and designs, and creative fonts. The screens are used to project lyrics and sermon notes but are also used as an added "transitional" tool, projecting interesting images. As worshipers move from one part of the service into another, they have something to hold their attention 100 percent of the time.

You may not have the immediate resources to do something so involved and there's nothing wrong with starting simply. In fact, if you are targeting postmoderns, who are more comfortable with technology than any other group, simplicity may be preferred anyway. At Warehouse 242, white letters on a black background with the congregation logo lightly superimposed is the signature style. Anything more than that is viewed by many people as a distraction. One Sunday, the PowerPoint technician decided to change the colors of the font and background to blue and yellow, and added an effect on the word *Lord* in the chorus, making that particular word appear to be spinning off the screen. Rarely does anyone comment on the PowerPoint from week to week, but, to this day, snide remarks are still being heard about the "swirling Lord." Moral of the story: Know your audience!

Visual arts

The room or building where you meet can provide a visually stimulating setting that reflects the life, values, and personality of your worshiping community and draws newcomers in. Look for opportunities to display

Projecting the words enables us to keep our noses out of worship folders and hymnals.

original paintings, sculpture, and framed poetry in areas where people mingle and talk while they enjoy the art together.

At Warehouse 242, banners depicting the five core values of the church are displayed at every service. Each one was painted by a different person, two of whom still have fully not embraced the message of the gospel, but who know our community as a place where they are free to be "in process." Inviting them to express their artistic abilities in a tangible way that contributes to the community was just as important as the finished work.

Take a fresh look at what may already be right under your noses, such as stained-glass windows, stations-of-the-cross sculptures, symbols, icons, and paintings. Just because they are traditional or familiar doesn't mean they are irrelevant. Breathe new life into the foundations of our faith by creating new, visual ways to signal holy days and seasons of the church year. Use these new works of art to tie the present to the past.

See CD
Resource
5A

CD Resource 5A illustrates how a group of artists at Warehouse 242 put together an action plan for arts in the congregation. Use it to spark ideas for your setting.

God calls us

No doubt, the task feels daunting, especially to congregational leaders who come from traditions with prescribed forms of worship. And there may even be some people in your midst who are resistant to such change. Truth is, God's heartbeat is for those who are lost and, therefore, we too must bleed concern for our friends and neighbors who have not yet experienced this amazing grace for themselves. If God has called us to this task, then God will surely provide the resources we need do it.

The world—and your community—is full of people like my friend Lisa who are ready to be wooed by a God who relentlessly pursues us, whose full expression is one of beauty and joy. I now have a place where I can eagerly and unhesitatingly take "Lisas" of today. It is a place set apart but at the same time inviting and familiar and holds some elements in common with the world they know; a place that connects their own story to God's greater story—the story that will forever satisfy their deepest longings and desires. Your congregation can be that place, too.

CHAPTER 6

Preaching That Reaches Members and Guests

William Bartlett

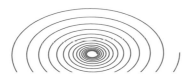

In the previous chapter, the writer shared her struggle to find a worship service that would present Jesus Christ to her friend Lisa in a relevant and an effective manner. While chapter 5 explored several art forms and media through which the gospel can be effectively communicated, this chapter narrows the focus of communicating the gospel to the sermon, the preached word of God, and one of the hallmarks of Lutheran worship.

We wish to see Jesus

The following illustration aptly describes the purpose of the preached word of God.

A little girl and her father faithfully attended worship every week at their home church. The father would dutifully escort his daughter to the front row, hoping that her attention would stay focused on the pastor and others leading worship. The girl loved the worship service and the setting. The beautiful mosaic of Jesus facing the congregation warmed the little girl's heart week after week. One Sunday, the father and daughter arrived,

---

William Bartlett has served as pastor of Lutheran Church of the Cross, Laguna Woods, California, since 1990. He loves talking to others about Jesus Christ and God's word.

sat in the front row, and were surprised to see a guest preacher step into the pulpit. This guest preacher was diminutive in build in contrast to their regular pastor, who was very tall and broad. After the sermon, the girl leaned over to her father and said, "I like this pastor! He lets me see Jesus!"

The goal of preaching is to exhibit Jesus, not expound him. The Bible tells of a time when some outsiders came to Philip the Disciple, and said, "Sir, we wish to see Jesus" (John 12:21). P. T. Forsyth, a great early twentieth-century British preacher, wrote, "Christ exhibited God, He did not expound Him. He was His witness, not His apologist. He did more to reveal than to interpret" (*Spiritual Classics,* Augsburg, 1990, p. 271).

The guest preacher exhibited Christ most clearly, not through his words, but through his presence—or, more accurately, his lack of presence. Is that not also the goal in preaching—to exhibit Christ and to erase ourselves?

> God's word, not our words, bring about salvation and healing.

Preaching is important; the preacher is not

The awesome responsibility of prescribing and administering medicine to a sick or dying patient with, at most, temporal ramifications is frightening. But being charged with the responsibility of delivering the life-saving message of the gospel to a sin-sick and dying world, with eternal ramifications, is nothing short of terrifying.

Preachers can find reassurance knowing that it is God's word, not our words, that bring about salvation and healing. The Lord revels in using inarticulate, unlikely, and even impure means by which to convey saving grace. Moses, the slow-of-speech ambassador to Pharaoh; Balaam's donkey; the apostle Peter, with all his imperfections and sins; and even an inanimate burning bush all effectively delivered God's word.

The preached word of God is powerful and effective in its own strength and ability, not in the eloquence, style, or purity of its delivery. That realization saved me and allowed me entrance into the ministry and pulpit. If God's word could bring the entire 120,000 population of the city of Nineveh to repentance through the reluctant and lackluster preaching of Jonah, then the Lord can use me and other imperfect humans, too.

When people—guests and members alike—come to church, they wish to see Jesus. So, preach the word, exhibit Christ, and get out of the way!

Assumptions for preaching

Consider the following assumptions as a guide to the content and delivery of the preached word.

1. Everybody hurts in some way—due to guilt, anger, illness, strained relationships, despair, or sin. Strive to look at each person in the congregation with the compassionate eyes of Jesus.

2. There are both believers and unbelievers in the congregation—and it is not up to the preacher to judge for certain which is which. Judgment alone belongs to the Lord. However, the mere fact that both believers and nonbelievers are present makes the preaching-moment a critically important opportunity.

In the book *Perelandra,* C. S. Lewis wrote about making the most of every preaching opportunity because worship is one venue through which eternal destinations may change. Lewis suggested that, though there are "a thousand roads" by which one can walk through this world, there is not one such road that does not eventually lead to either heaven or hell (London: The Bodley Heave, 1943). Because it is a vehicle of God's word, every sermon is an opportunity to experience God's saving grace.

3. Any sermon can be used by God. If God's word is the substance of a prayerfully and diligently prepared message and if it is delivered with a heart fully given to the Lord, there can never be a bad sermon. Just as the Lord's Supper is not rendered ineffective by a poor wine and baptism is not voided by dirty water, so preaching is made effective by the word of God, not the preacher.

4. Preaching is a vehicle of grace. In Romans 10:14, Paul tells us, "How can they believe in the one of whom they have not heard? And how can they hear without someone preaching to them?" (NIV). God ordained the preached word as a promised means of imparting a saving faith. This promise gives us courage and confidence to preach.

5. God's word never returns empty (Isaiah 55:11). God's word behind my own words has made effective many imperfect attempts at imparting a saving message.

6. Someone may be opened to receiving God's saving grace through the miracle and power of the preached word. A visitor stood in line on his way

> **There can never be a bad sermon.**

out of church one Sunday and asked the pastor if this was the church in which his friend, whom he named, was saved a couple of weeks earlier. The pastor, not comfortable with such evangelical language, replied, "I don't think so. People don't get saved here. They just come to worship." May our preaching be pregnant with the possibility of salvation through the power of God's word in our words!

7. *God's word feeds our souls.* Just as we do not need to be able to recall what we have eaten for our bodies to be nourished, our sermons do not need to be remembered for God's word, through our sermons, to feed souls and transform lives.

8. *The primary goal in preaching is to proclaim Christ* and him crucified (1 Corinthians 2:2). The simple message of Christ-crucified needs to be present somewhere, and this message is more important and effective than the best joke or illustration.

> **The primary goal in preaching is to proclaim Christ and him crucified.**

9. God's word invites a response—so should the sermon. Therefore, include in every sermon an application from Scripture for Christian discipleship or an invitation to submit more of one's life to the Lord.

10. Your preaching is not that important; God's word is.

Preaching styles, patterns, and techniques

With our ever-escalating ability to confront a crowd with multimedia messages and Microsoft® PowerPoint® presentations, old-fashioned preaching may seem ineffective and powerless. However, biblical theology and the power of God's word testified to throughout Scripture remind us that substance is always more important than style. Nevertheless, it is incumbent upon us, due to the worthiness of the message and the task, to take preaching seriously and to present our preaching, in a deserving manner, as an offering to the Lord.

Delivery styles

There are several styles of delivering sermons beyond the traditional, and still valid, exegetical or didactic model. Practicing a variety of preaching styles in worship services on a regular basis will increase not only effectiveness for unchurched guests, but also freshness and impact on a potentially complacent congregation.

Narrative preaching. Narrative preaching is simply retelling a Bible story. Who can improve upon "The Greatest Story Ever Told"? There is wisdom and validity in just retelling the great stories, parables, and miracles of the Bible to both the long-term member and the first-time guest.

Dialogue sermons. Dialogue sermons often spark interest and response because of the novelty of two or more people doing what is usually done by one person. The variety of voices, views, and venues often involved in a dialogue sermon combines to make it an excellent occasional model of preaching.

First-person narrative preaching. A first-person narrative, like a drama, is another potentially powerful way to proclaim God's word. Differentiated from chancel drama, which often involves more elaborate sets, scripts, people, and rehearsals, this is a simple, dramatic, first-person impersonation. Biblical characters and influential disciples from Christian history can be effectively portrayed in the first-person with costuming ranging from very simple to ornate.

Smaller congregations—including guests—tend to be generous in accepting considerably less than Oscar-winning performances. In fact, small congregations are often grateful for the effort. In larger congregations, however, it is more likely critics will be present and the expectation for excellence will be higher.

Sermon series

In attempting to reach an unchurched population in a community, many pastors and congregations are discovering the value of occasional preaching series.

Topical series. Short-sermon series, lasting from two to eight weeks and dealing with topics that affect or afflict believers and nonbelievers alike, are helpful evangelism tools. Sermon series can address a multitude of topics from marriage and parenting to financial management and stress reduction. Introducing a topical series usually will mean a departure from lectionary-based sermons, which follow the liturgical year.

Bible book or chapter series. Another form of sermon series is not based on topics, but rather on books or chapters from the Bible. For example, a several-week series on Jesus' Sermon on the Mount (in Matthew 5-7), or a several-month excursion through any one of the apostle

Practicing a variety of preaching styles will increase freshness and impact.

Paul's many letters brings a welcome continuity to new Christians who do not yet have a full grasp of what is coming in the liturgical year. This kind of series can effectively make use of the appointed readings from the Sunday lectionary.

Christian book series. A book with Christian themes can be used as the basis of a sermon series. The best book preaching-series our congregation ever experienced was based on Charles Sheldon's classic book, *In His Steps.* This book faithfully captivated the congregation and confronted them with the power of God's word. We did this series during the seven-week season of Easter, assigning one or two chapters per week for congregational reading and then focusing on those chapters in the sermon each Sunday. The "experiment" in the plot of the book—that of attempting to "walk in his steps"—became our congregation's experiment during that time.

> The possibility of using multimedia enhancements, such as Microsoft ® PowerPoint ®, is present in virtually every congregation.

Adding punch to the proclamation

Here are three examples of ways to accentuate a sermon.

- *Microsoft ® PowerPoint ® presentations.* With the proliferation of computers and technically-adept members across all geographical, cultural, and economic boundaries, the possibility of using multimedia enhancements, such as PowerPoint, is present in virtually every congregation. The software programs and hardware necessary for computer-graphics video projection are becoming more and more affordable and are relatively simple to use. Whether the computer graphics display highlights words from the biblical text for the day, an image, or a short MPEG (Moving Picture Expert Group) video clip, this visual aid can add impact to the message.

- *Drama.* There are abundant published resources full of dramas specifically written for church worship use. These short skits or dramas, often lasting only four to six minutes, are finding enthusiastic acceptance in all sizes and stripes of congregations. They are effective means of introducing a theme or a topic to be addressed in the day's sermon or service. Willow Creek Community Church, Barrington, Illinois, uses drama successfully and publishes such dramas for other congregations' use.

• *Sermon outlines or notes.* A simple but valuable enhancement to preaching is the use of sermon notes. Usually printed on half-page inserts in the worship folder, these outlines of the day's message are a helpful means of holding people's attention during the sermon. Often, the preacher will leave blanks in the outline for the worshiper to fill in with his or her own responses or to simply fill in words that are found in the day's message. This added involvement by the worshipers not only helps keep attention focused, but it also enhances learning by integrating additional senses and involvement in the sermon beyond just hearing and seeing. The sermon outline also provides a helpful template on which the preacher can organize thoughts and craft a sermon that contextualizes the message (introduction), cradles the gospel (God's word), and challenges the hearer (application). See the accompanying CD Resources 6A and 6B for an example of a sermon outline and a sermon evaluation form.

See CD Resources

Internet sites showcasing technological capabilities

For some fine examples of advanced use of technology in preaching, visit the following churches' Web sites and navigate within the sites to resources for preaching, such as dramas or sermon outlines, or to archived sermons—complete with audio, video, PowerPoint, and even MPEG graphics. You can download the sermons and experience the full audio, video, and technical special effects of the original sermon, including congregational response—just as if you were a guest in worship at that church. Several of these sites are churches that intentionally program and preach to reach specific generational groups, such as baby boomers, baby busters, Generation Xers, and postmoderns. The icon in the margin directs you to CD Resource 6D, which shows what these Web sites look like and how technology can be used for preaching and reaching people for Christ.

See CD Resource 6D

Community Church of Joy, Phoenix, Arizona
www.joyonline.org

Ginhamsburg United Methodist Church, Tipp City, Ohio
www.ginghamsburg.org

Prince of Peace Lutheran Church, Burnsville, Minnesota
www.princeofpeaceonline.org

Willow Creek Community Church, South Barrington, Illinois
www.willowcreek.org

Preparing for preaching

The preparation of a sermon is a multifaceted process involving a balance of prayer, exegetical study, contextualization, preparation, pruning, and practice. Below is a ten-step process to guide the development of a sermon from the Scripture text to the heart of the worshiper. Refer to the accompanying CD-ROM for a worksheet containing these ten steps. See CD Resource 6C.

Step 1: Pray. Pray that what is to be prepared may be faithful to Christ and God's word and used by the Lord for the furtherance of the kingdom of God. "May the words of my mouth and the meditation of my heart be pleasing in your sight, O LORD, my Rock and my Redeemer" (Psalm 19:14, NIV).

Step 2: Read. First, read the Bible passage upon which you will preach. Next, read related texts to this passage. If possible, do language study on the preaching text. Finally, read commentaries, other sermons, and search for illustrative and corroborating materials. See CD Resources 6E and 6F for an illustration of source material available through Bible Explorer and other similar electronic resources.

Step 3: Identify the point about God's word to be made in the sermon. Write it down in a concise statement or sermon title. Make sure everything written or spoken in the sermon supports this truth.

Step 4: Contextualize the material. Use the examples, word choices, preaching style, preaching location (pulpit, podium, or platform), and delivery style (formal or casual) that will most effectively communicate God's word to those in the congregation.

Step 5: Acknowledge the essential and necessary. This relates to contextualizing the message but has more to do with current events than local culture. If something newsworthy has just happened or is happening (such as a local, national, or international disaster or incident) acknowledge it—even if just briefly—because not to do so would be either an offense to those present or a stumbling block to the message you are attempting to proclaim.

Step 6: Avoid jargon. Refrain from cultural, class, generational, ethnic, or "insider" jargon if you are preaching to a congregation with even a slight degree of diversity.

Step 7: Use variation. Vary the style, pattern, and techniques of the message and the delivery of the message over the course of the year.

Step 8: "Jesus proof" the message. Read through the manuscript or notes to look for frequent reference to the person and name of Jesus Christ. Read the first few chapters of the book of Acts as a baseline model for preaching in the name of Christ.

Step 9: Practice delivering the sermon. Read through your notes or manuscript several times in order to become so familiar with the message that conviction and sincerity worthily permeate its delivery.

Step 10: Pray. Pray that what is said may bring honor and glory to the Lord, and that it may equally bring Jesus Christ and the transforming gospel to the listener. "Pray that I may proclaim [the mystery of Christ] clearly, as I should . . . make the most of every opportunity" (Colossians 4:3-4, NIV).

Pray that what is to be prepared may be faithful to Christ and God's word.

The most important gift a preacher can give the congregation, guest and member, is Jesus. Let them see Jesus. Don't just expound him, exhibit him! "And how can they believe in the one of whom they have not heard? And how can they hear without someone preaching to them?" (Romans 10:14, NIV).

CHAPTER 7

Worship Planning and Implementation

Terri Bocklund McLean

There's an enormous difference between driving a nail and designing a building. One can have all the tools necessary, but without a good set of plans, the tools aren't much help. The subject of this chapter is the architecture of worship that reaches out—the importance of careful planning that recognizes widening the circle doesn't happen by accident. Questions pertinent and familiar to congregational leaders and planners are used as section headings throughout this chapter. These are questions for congregations to consider as they engage in the process of designing worship that reaches.

Exploring a new worship evangelism strategy

In a new worship evangelism strategy, it is not only prudent but truly visionary to begin with the end in mind. By envisioning the fruits of an effective worship evangelism strategy, you ultimately see more and new people worshiping with you. But how do you reach this goal? The first question to consider is about who those new people are.

Terri Bocklund McLean has served as a musician and worship leader in three congregations with a mission of evangelical outreach. She is the author of New Harmonies *(Alban Institute, 1998).*

Whom is this new worship evangelism strategy for?

This is a mission question! If it isn't for the sake of those who are not worshiping with you today, then you are merely creating an alternative for the entrenched faithful, not a mission outpost for a hurting world that needs a savior. Research shows that the first meaningful point of contact congregations are likely to make with an unchurched neighbor is through worship opportunities—not a pie social, not a youth event, and certainly not a fundraiser. The whole point of worship evangelism is a spiritual one—helping people to build a relationship with the triune God. To that end, it's critical that entry into the worship life of a congregation is easy and open.

Begin with the end in mind.

Leonard Sweet, a church-health expert for our times, has suggested that to be truly evangelical today, worship needs to be more than relevant or contemporary. We need to make worship an EPIC event that is, week in and week out, *experiential, participatory, image-based,* and *connective.* Sweet has updated this acronym from an earlier version in which *interactive* and *communal*, rather than *image-based* and *connective,* were two of the four operative words (*Soul Tsunami,* Zondervan, 1999). This is at once an ancient and a radically contemporary concept. It frees us from believing that there is only one formula for successful congregational outreach. It points to complexity and diversity, while reinforcing the importance of understanding context.

Once you have a picture of who you want to reach, it's time to ask some questions about your congregation.

Are we ready yet?

A congregation is ready for worship that reaches when:

- the congregation calls those with unfamiliar faces "first-time worshipers" or "guests," not "visitors."
- the congregation knows that making disciples is more important than making members.
- the resistance toward doing new things (or old things in a new way) takes a backseat to a vision for mission.
- hospitality becomes a worship issue, not merely an issue of name tags, greeters, and doughnuts.

Who needs to know among our faith community?

As congregations consider transforming their worship planning processes to make the most of worship's evangelical potential, pastors and other leaders cast the vision before the people. They do this first in casual conversations, well before it's discussed in meetings. Leaders take the opportunity to talk with church-goers about questions, such as "From your perspective, what would happen if more people were here for worship?" and "What would we need to do to accommodate them?" These answers help you to know what it will take to commit to a new worship evangelism strategy that is not an experiment; a strategy that may take more planning time and more work than "the way we've always done it." It also helps create a "who needs to know" list that will be useful as implementation begins and as a team is formed. (See CD Resource 7A for a tool to record responses.)

See CD
Resource
7A

Leaders are in the best position to know the stakeholders who are spread over the landscape of congregational life. It is best that these stakeholders be brought on board at the earliest possible opportunity when changes are being contemplated for ministry, programs, and planning. This is especially true when those changes affect worship. It's important not to miss these folks in the conversations at this early exploration stage. The benefits are two-fold: every niche of congregational life has had an opportunity to weigh-in on changes, thus feeling they have been heard and their ideas are valued. And leaders know what problems and land mines might lie before them as change is undertaken.

As you collect answers to these questions, present them to the congregation in order to gather enthusiasm, momentum, unity, and resolve behind this mission-oriented change to worship and the planning process. Use any preferred method for distributing such information, such as by newsletter, written announcement in the worship bulletin, spoken announcement during worship, e-mail announcement, or congregational meeting.

Who needs to know in our neighborhood?

This is a question of facility preparedness and entrances and exits to the property. Again, beginning with the end in mind and envisioning more and new people at every worship opportunity, leaders ask:

- Do adjacent landowners need to know about additional flow of traffic, outdoor events, or changes to church property?
- Does zoning need to change?
- It's best to have excellent relationships with those who use or own adjacent properties.

Who has already been where we are going?

One of the most grievous situations in the church today is the resistance among faith communities to connect and network with each other. Congregations in your area who have been where you want to go can provide "road maps" and inspiration, and help you avoid the pitfalls of change. Perhaps the most important question you can ask those who have been where you want to go is: What didn't work as you undertook your change and why?

With the World Wide Web redefining the meaning of *neighbor*, it's important not to overlook our virtual neighbors in the faith community. Many congregations make it part of their mission to share their story and information. They make themselves a resource via the Internet to help congregations in transition. These congregations have terrific Web sites and can be reached on-line. Some of these congregations host conferences to provide guidance and assistance to changing churches. A brief list of these congregations can be found in the Resource List on pages 106-112.

Congregations in your area who have been where you want to go can provide "road maps."

Implementing a new strategy

The need for an Implementation Team arises when the initial exploration has been done and people start asking, "What's next?" The Implementation Team serves as a bridge between fundamental fact-finding and putting a new planning strategy into motion. This team gathers around the question "How will we get where we are going?" When the work of the Implementation Team is finished, they pass the baton to the team that will lead worship.

Who needs to be on the Implementation Team?

Besides the pastor(s), membership on this team will include as many in the following list as apply for your context:

Examine the
connections
between
the worship
evangelism
task and the
congregation's
mission
statement.

- leaders of music ministries and anyone involved in leading other liturgical arts ministries such as drama, dance, and visual arts
- lay leaders or other church staff
- worship committee chair
- congregation president
- people who are excited about the future
- people who have worshiped elsewhere and have ideas and enthusiasm for doing something new
- altar guild chair

A "minister of sight and sound"—someone familiar with sound systems and computer graphics—might also be included, as well as someone familiar with the church's architectural features, lighting, and electrical wiring. Refer to the "Who Needs to Know" list you compile early in the process to make certain all bases have been covered.

What is the mission of the Implementation Team?

See CD
Resource
7B

Members of the team examine the congregation's mission statement and create its purpose statement as an offshoot of the congregational mission statement. (See CD Resource 7B, "Implementation Team Mission-Statement Workshop.") When the work of the team can be directly related to an already-existing mission statement, more people can see that work as a mission opportunity for the congregation to move toward together. If the team's purpose and task have been determined by another body, such as the congregation council, it is still worthwhile for the group to examine the connections between their worship evangelism task and the congregation's mission statement.

An essential part of this team's ministry is praying for the mission, for one another as ministers to the mission, for the congregation, and for the community surrounding the congregation. Understanding the work of this group as a "ministry team" rather than a "task team" means that every gathering includes worshiping together—praising, sharing, and praying together. This way the team stays spiritually accountable to one another and to the congregation.

What is God calling the congregation to build?

The next order of business for the Implementation Team to consider is whether a linear versus a nonlinear style for planning is right for you. If you understand the last sentence, it might be your first clue that a more nonlinear approach is the right fit. If you don't get it, not to worry— a linear style is perfectly fine! What is important is to understand the people you intend to reach so that you choose a worship planning approach that suits them.

Linear planning puts worship strategies in a straight line, with point A (for example, choosing the preaching text) then point B (for example, selecting the hymns), and so on, with the ultimate goal of getting to "the end of the line" weekly, as you arrive each week at your Sabbath. Linear planning may be well-suited for faith communities that want to appeal to the World War II generation or older baby boomers. It's a strategy that keeps ideas about worship flowing in a fairly predictable method, with the ultimate worship structure offering some sameness ("tradition," old or new) from week to week. Elements of the worship service remain in a predictable order, and the execution of service elements and creative changes happen within that order.

Nonlinear worship planning and the nonlinear worship style that follows could be considered more cyclical, with more surprises, and consequently more appealing to younger or less traditional members, who often find the more linear style too predictable or stiff, and who may, over time, call it uninteresting and unengaging. Planning in the nonlinear style is raw and organic, more like a creation than a recipe, and less attached to tradition.

Most congregations will have some elements of linear and nonlinear styles in their planning strategies, but one of these styles might be a better match the people you want to reach.

What must be planned each week, month, and year?

The answer to this question depends entirely on whether your congregation's worship evangelism strategy will lean towards a linear or nonlinear approach. Timeline worksheets for both linear and nonlinear planning are available on the CD-ROM as CD Resource 7C.

See CD
Resource
7C

Whose stories must we hear as we proceed?

Rev. Robert Wallace at St. John Evangelical Lutheran Church in Columbia, Maryland, suggests that listening to stories is perhaps the most important work a ministry team can do together.

First, Wallace asserts, listen to the God story together through Bible study. This is central to understanding God's will and God's work in the midst of the faith community. Assume that there is biblical illiteracy in the ranks. Instead of straining under the reality of it, work with it in the midst of every ministry of the congregation.

Second, strive to hear the story of the surrounding community through its history and its leaders. A huge piece of community identity can be understood through the story of place.

Third, hear the story of your congregation—its history, personality, leaders, battles, and baggage. These stories can reveal much about its systems and its modus operandi.

Fourth, it is a blessing to all when you listen to one another's personal faith stories. All these stories can gracefully inform the work of worship planning.

Who are prospects in our community?

It makes good sense to have a general picture of who might drift through your doorways for worship. It's easy enough to discover what music stations are most popular, what are the general income levels, and what type of homes and home-buyers are nearby. Is our neighborhood primarily composed of first time home-owners? Renters? Farmers? Empty-nesters? Singles? Established families?

See chapter 3 for more information on understanding context. Knowing who might someday be in your midst informs many decisions of the Implementation Team. Otherwise, you could end up making worship decisions based on the preferences of those who are already there instead of the local neighbors you want to reach. One represents the attitude of a religious club, while the other represents evangelism.

Knowing who might someday be in your midst informs many decisions.

What existing groups do we need to connect with?

All of them! This question is important not only in the planning stages, but for ongoing planning as well. You can never ask, "Who needs to know?" often enough. Since changes can sometimes create divisions in congregations, honoring and respecting other congregational ministries by doing an enormous amount of checking-in and bridge-building with them is smart. No guarantee can be made that all participants in all ministries will be willing to lend their wholehearted support to the change process. If you invite input and take time to listen, those who dissent might not harbor the kind of resentment or hurt that gains its own momentum and leads to an unhealthy undercurrent in the congregation.

How will resources be selected?

This question alone merits an entire chapter—and one exists! Saying "yes" and "no" to what's available for the church's worship is an important job that requires an informed theology as well as sensitivity to what fits the congregation. Before purchasing them and plugging them into worship, resources should be carefully examined for content and appropriateness—especially music lyrics and translations of traditional worship materials such as creeds and confessions. Essentially, it is best if someone is appointed the task of reviewing resources and then recommending their purchase based on two essential items of critique.

First, worship resources should tell the truth as the congregation preaches it. Second, these resources should be shaped into a form that people will understand, whether the form is musical style or phrasing of congregational spoken material. Chapter 4 addresses selection criteria in detail.

How will we evaluate our effectiveness?

A tool for short-term evaluation is found in CD Resource 7D on the CD-ROM. "Worship Evaluation Continuum" can help identify the attributes of an ideal worship service for your congregation.

Whether you plan in a linear or nonlinear style, also evaluate worship by using "Weekly EPIC Planning for Worship That Reaches," CD Resource 7E. It is designed to help leaders see where strengths and growing edges lie.

See CD
Resources

Long-term evaluation can be done most effectively by assembling focus groups and asking them to consider the same worksheet, but rather than evaluating the previous week, have them review the last church season or quarter (three months). Getting the perspective of worshipers enhances leaders' ability to see the "big picture."

Who will lead the way?

The work of the people begins in the planning stages.

Beyond the work of the Implementation Team lies the territory of fueling and tracking the week-to-week adventure of worship planning. Too often, pastors hold all the keys to worship planning, from selecting hymns and songs to directing acolytes. Liturgy is not only accomplished in the midst of worship, the work of the people begins in the planning stages. For every ministry that contributes gifts of time, talent, and leadership, a representative of that ministry should be present and empowered for worship planning. Worship planning might then include not only the pastor but also the organist, the choir director, the person who will change the paraments and hang the new banner, the leader of the drama team, and the praise band leader.

The EPIC worship planning strategy

See CD Resource 7E

Use CD Resource 7E on the CD-ROM, entitled "Weekly EPIC Planning for Worship That Reaches," to be certain that worship is planned with EPIC qualities in mind. As you use the worksheet arm yourself with the following information.

Experiential

Ask yourselves these questions:
- How will people use their senses?
- How will they experience a change of atmosphere or mood, and to what specifically and emotionally will they respond?

Worship for the age in which we live must be an honest-to-goodness God experience. A garden center in suburban Baltimore used to advertise itself as a "must-see"; it now advertises itself as a "must-experience." It gets what the church desperately needs to understand. Worship needs to be planned to become more multisensory than it has in centuries. It needs to become a holy barrage of the senses and the self. It needs to be an event that engages us on every level and assures us when we have completed that time we have really been through something vital and alive. For too long the church worship experience has been very short on the five-senses experience, focusing mainly on the visual and the auditory. Typically, we don't smell much or touch much, and even the tasting we engage in during our best naturally-EPIC element, the Eucharist, is too frequently the tasteless wafer and the most carefully meted-out sip of grape juice or wine.

An experience, in the postmodern sense of the word, awakens us completely, on all levels of our person. Beyond the physical senses, we are awakened to and engage the spiritual, emotional, and intellectual sides of ourselves as well. There's good news here for the church. Hanging around with Jesus Christ was certainly an experience, according to Matthew, Mark, Luke, and John. If we, the church today, are the body of Christ, then we have the best possible advantage in offering a real experience in our worship life! Imagine the power that would be unleashed if the culture were to be awakened to, apprehended, and connected to the church as the experience of Christ!

An experience awakens us completely, on all levels of our person.

Participatory

Consider these questions:
- What can we ask a worshiper to do that the pastor or another worship leader usually does?
- How can our leaders get out of the way?

Worship that reaches out is a participatory adventure. No one is a bystander, no one is an observer, and no one is being simply taught or entertained. The boundary between leader and congregant is blurred by effective welcome and invitation. Postmodern believers, and as it turns out, even postmodern seekers, would rather be part of the telling of a story than be told a story; would rather be in an experience that changes them than be told how to change; would rather be given a moment of freedom to choose and offer unique responses than read a proscribed one in concert with everyone else, hearing their own voices disappear.

Image–based

Ask yourselves these questions:
- What will the worshiper see that will enrich the worship time?
- How will humor be a part of the service?

More than ever, our world has become a visual world. Meaning is enhanced, layer upon layer, by what is seen. When the question "What are you doing to save time?" is asked, all by itself, it is a rather flat mental experience. But imagine that question enhanced by this visual image: a kitchen counter stacked high with dirty dinner dishes—one of those double sinks, the right side of it full to overflowing with water and dirty dishes, and the left side full to overflowing with water and a naked baby, with a look of surprise on its little face! The question is no longer a flat mental experience. Even without visual illustration, the mind fills in the blanks and creates an image that enhances meaning. The meanings and messages of the gospel are ripe for using powerful visuals as bridging elements to deeper understanding and application to everyday life.

Visuals, whether they are high-tech or low-tech, enhance meaning and engage the whole person. Still-life arrangements of ordinary and readily available objects that connect to Scripture and sermon themes are equally as effective as projected images that are professionally produced. Consider the simple yet powerful visual message of a smiling face: warm, friendly churches have smiling faces in the parking lot, at the door, in the pulpit, and in the pews. See the many excellent original video products for worship available at www.ginghamsburg.org and listed under the headings "Film and video" and "Photography" of the Resource List on pages 111-112.

Equally important to worship that reaches is the presence of humor during worship. Whether planned or spontaneous, laughter is a gift that people take home with them and makes community time memorable. Humor can be introduced effectively in storytelling during sermons and in dramas.

Connective

Consider these questions:
- How will worshipers touch and be touched?
- How will they connect to someone else mentally, emotionally, and spiritually?

We live in a culture that is becoming increasingly touch-deprived, or human-contact-deprived. Things we used to accomplish by engaging with another human being we can now do from the comfort of our cars, kitchen tables, or computer terminals. The result is a culture starving for what we are hard-wired to need—touch, contact points, being heard and being known. In EPIC churches, we decide to be "entrenched transactors"—like the folks who still go to the teller window inside the bank to get cash instead of using the ATM, or the folks who drive through the toll booth staffed by a live body even when they have the correct change, just to say "Hello, have a nice day!" The church can never become completely automated, and we need to carefully craft and plan for one-to-one interactions with others for each and every Sunday.

These encounters need to be appropriate, safe, and meaningful. Prince of Peace Lutheran Church in Burnsville, Minnesota, has a wonderfully connective "green dot" ministry. Each week during worship, prayer requests are written down and brought forward. Anyone who wants to commit to praying for one of these prayer requests takes the paper on which it is written, along with a small green adhesive dot. The green dot is placed on the center of the person's watch. Every time the worshiper checks the time during the next week, there is the green-dot reminder to pray. Green means "go" in a life of prayer, just as it means "go" on the roadways. All week, the spiritual connection between two people remains alive and vital through one simple green dot.

We live in a culture that is becoming increasingly touch-deprived.

Ideas for smaller congregations

Planning for worship that reaches depends upon the resources you have at hand, especially people resources. Small-membership congregations need not despair that the ideas presented here only work in bigger congregations with lots of people and money. Here are some ideas for leaders of small congregations to consider.

If you don't and can't offer several worship services, each with a different worship style, try to incorporate creative worship components on a weekly basis in your existing worship services. Or change the style of worship on a seasonal basis.

If people resources for a worship leadership team are limited, start small. If you organize a new group, have them begin by leading a one-time event, such as vacation Bible school. One rural Minnesota congregation is beginning this way with a team of high-school youth. Or call on an existing choir or part of the choir to take on a new role in a new service.

The latest technology is not required to create an EPIC experience. The ideas that follow can lead to low budget but high impact results!

EPIC and the Worship Leadership Team

We know that the story of our servant Savior cannot become truer or more vital. So as members of your Worship Leadership Team receive the baton and move toward a new strategy of worship evangelism, their task lies in envisioning how worship of that Savior might become more EPIC. CD Resource 7F, "EPIC Evaluation," on the CD-ROM is a helpful tool early in the transition to new and effective worship planning strategies. It is also an excellent prompt for ongoing worship planning that incorporates, maintains, and nourishes an EPIC vitality in the worship life of a congregation.

See CD
Resource
7F

Using "EPIC Evaluation," have the Worship Leadership Team undertake an inventory of the current quality of worship as it relates to EPIC worship planning strategies. The worksheet will help you identify how your current worship service is experiential, participatory, image-based, and connective and how it can become more so. Identify areas of strengths as well as the experimental or growing edges.

Ideally worship that reaches never gets bogged down, nailed down, or weighed down. When the Worship Leadership Team continues to ask the EPIC questions, it will inevitably find itself becoming more skillful in its task, becoming more empowered to answer creatively, and seeing farther down the pathway toward worship that reaches. Its faithful pursuit of the task results in a congregation discovering itself to be the church God has equipped it to be—the body of Jesus Christ, given for all.

CHAPTER 8

Music Leadership

Tom Frodsham

Building an effective music leadership team for worship can be a lot like sailing to a new world. First you must have a destination (vision), a captain (leader), and a crew (music team). In addition, you will want a compass (accountability through prayer, Scripture, and pastoral involvement), good rigging (music), and the ability to feed the crew (Bible study and mutual support). Most important, you need the wind (Holy Spirit) and sails (open hearts and minds) to catch the wind.

Catching the wind

For hearts and minds to be open to God's leading in this new ministry venture, prayer, congregation support, and a clear vision of where you are headed are essential.

Prayer

Before you make any great plans, find the best music, and recruit the most gifted musicians, turn to God in prayer. God already is already at work, has inspired the best music, and has gifted people who are waiting to be asked to participate. Through prayer, ask God to lead and to guide you. Pray for God to call people into this ministry. Pray for God to inspire your

---

Tom Frodsham is director of music ministries at Bethlehem Lutheran Church, Marysville, Washington, and a congregational worship consultant.

congregation and its leaders and pray that God would keep your motives pure. Ego can be a giant monster in the seas of music leadership, and God is the one that can keep that monster at bay.

To discern God's intent for this venture, listen patiently and be open. If you meet someone who might be interested, get their phone number. The Holy Spirit speaks to us when and where we least expect it.

Congregation support

Talk about how this new ministry fits the overall vision for your church.

The planning team for worship has already sought congregational support. Continue the conversation with people in the congregation. If you are not the pastor, you need to be spending as much time as you can with the pastor. Time in prayer and time talking about how this new ministry fits into the overall vision for your church are essential. Keep communication open and going.

Vision

At the point of gathering the music leadership team, your congregation and its leaders will have defined the vision for this ministry, who it is you are trying to reach, and the kind of music that you think will contribute to the worship experience of these guests. Be sure you have this information in hand as you gather the music team.

The captain

The qualities listed below can assist you, the pastor(s) and worship committee members, in choosing a worship-music leader. If you are that leader, search your heart as you read this section on the attributes of a good leader.

Love of God and neighbor

The greatest commandment of worship leading is this: Love the Lord your God with all your heart, soul, and mind (Matthew 22:37). This may sound obvious; a solid faith foundation and love of God are essential to strong leadership. And the second is like it: Love your neighbor as yourself (Matthew 22:39). This includes people who are late, disruptive, and ego-driven, and people who live lives you don't agree with. It also includes those who hold political views different from yours and those with different tastes in music. This is an unconditional love, a Christ-like love.

Commitment to the vision

Whatever this new worship service looks like, the person leading worship music needs to understand that it is one piece in a bigger picture of congregational evangelism and mission. The leader must understand and be committed to the long-range vision of the congregation.

In it for the long haul

"I press on toward the goal for the prize of the heavenly call of God in Christ Jesus" (Philippians 3:14). Bear in mind the notion of delayed gratification. A seamlessly orchestrated worship-music team isn't created overnight. It will probably be at least six months before you see any forward motion, and at least a year before it takes hold. Keep your eye on the prize!

A healthy and intentional devotional life

It is important for a worship-music leader to stay grounded in Scripture daily. There are many good devotional books out there. Pastors can provide recommendations and encouragement to leaders.

Personal worship

Worshiping God daily is key, and a worship-music leader should feel comfortable worshiping God anytime. Maybe during your devotion time or on the drive to work, sing a song of praise to God. I like to sing the Doxology: "Praise God from whom all blessings flow" as I walk across the parking lot everyday. Sometimes the birds join me! "Praise Him all creatures here below," and some days as I watch the sun rise, the heavens seem to open. "Praise him above ye heavenly host." Just do it! Worship God daily. "Praise Father, Son and Holy Ghost!" (*Lutheran Book of Worship* 564).

Active intercessory prayer

This goes hand-in-hand with loving people. If you love someone, you pray for them. Even if you are having a hard time loving someone, pray for that person. Pray for specific needs in that person's life. If you pray for

The leader must understand and be committed to the long-range vision of the congregation.

someone daily, God will transform your life. You will be amazed at how deeply you can care about someone you don't even like. Pray for everyone on your team.

A servant attitude

Stay grounded in Scripture.

"The greatest among you become like the youngest and the leader like one who serves" (Luke 22:26). The worship-music leader is often treated like a star. Be careful and prayerful. Don't forget about that great monster called Ego.

A sense of humor

Never take yourself too seriously. Remember that it's God who really makes things happen. Laughter truly is the best medicine, and it can really help out when a rehearsal gets a little tense. Worship-music leaders need to be able to laugh at themselves.

Acknowledges mistakes

Humility is a wonderful virtue. People love to follow a humble leader. Your team can teach you more than you could imagine, if you admit when you are wrong.

A grateful leader

An effective leader of any kind needs to say "thank you" over and over. But keep it real, and be specific about what you are thanking people for. It's also a good idea to thank them publicly from time to time.

Not afraid to fail or to succeed

Fear can be the biggest obstacle to any ministry. Fear creates mountains, but faith moves them. To live in faith, you must be willing to risk. Consider the parable of the talents (Matthew 25:14-30). In this story, the master gives three servants money to invest. Well, investing can be a risky business and while two of the servants made a nice profit for the master, the third, afraid to risk losing the money, buried it.

We need to take risks in our music ministry. If we are faithful, we cannot fail in God's eyes. Some people are also afraid of success. Remember what happened to the "successful" servants? They were put in charge of more. More work, more responsibility, more pressure. Don't let the fear of success limit your vision.

Shares leadership

When a music ministry starts to become successful, it is a wonderful thing and should be celebrated. But the reality is, as more people get involved and the ministry grows, it can be overwhelming. You can't do it all. Moses faced this same problem. In Exodus 18:18, Jethro told Moses, "You will surely wear yourself out, both you and these people with you. For the task is too heavy for you; you cannot do it alone." The worship-music leader needs to look for others he or she can mentor into leadership. Multiply your ministry by training others to do what you do. If there are multiple leaders, there can be multiple worship teams. It is amazing what God can do when we are willing to share the ministry.

Train others to do what you do.

Adaptive and eager to learn

The most important thing to keep in mind here is that this ministry belongs to God. As the ministry unfolds, you will need to be flexible and adaptable in order to receive the inevitable surprises. Continue to stay open; look for opportunities to learn and grow. There are conferences and workshops all around the nation. Try to find others who are doing the same kind of ministry as you. Getting together with peers to share ideas and pray for each other can be a godsend.

Accountable

Nobody wants to be micro-managed, but we all need to be held accountable. If you look at this in a healthy way, it is truly a gift. A kite in the wind without a string to keep it grounded would soon be lost. As a worship leader, you can stay grounded through prayer, Scripture, and an honest relationship with your pastor, as well as other trusted brothers and sisters in Christ.

The crew

One of the first tasks of your worship-music leader will be to recruit musicians for the worship leadership team. He or she also will need to lead

Attributes of a worship-music leader:

- loves God and neighbor
- committed to the vision
- in it for the long haul
- a healthy and intentional devotional life
- daily personal worship
- active intercessory prayer
- a servant attitude

- a sense of humor
- acknowledges mistakes
- a grateful leader
- not afraid to fail or to succeed
- shares leadership
- adaptive and eager to learn
- accountable

and schedule rehearsals and create opportunities for building spiritual community among the team.

Recruiting

When you start your search for musicians, singers, and audiovisual technicians, a lot of questions will come up. How good do they have to be? Do they need to be mature Christians? What level of commitment should I expect from them? And the ever-popular, Where do I find them? The answers will vary widely depending upon your context. As you begin this process, stay open to the Spirit's leading. Here are some general parameters to use when putting the team together:

Skill level. You don't need the best of the best, but you will need people who will give their best and can play their instruments. You don't want to be teaching one person a G chord on the guitar while everyone else is waiting.

Christian maturity. It's important that they believe, but they don't need to be lifelong pillars of the faith. It can actually be very exciting to use the invitation to be part of a worship team as an invitation into the faith. One of my best memories as a worship leader is the day a keyboard player for one of my bands was baptized.

You can find these people anywhere. They may be members already or they may be friends or relatives of a member. You might find a high school student that plays an instrument or sings. Get the word out that you are looking. Make sure that you and others are praying for God to send the right people.

Try to find someone connected to the local music scene. There are a lot of talented players out there who work in bars or nightclubs and are looking for a more meaningful way to use their gifts. Don't be afraid to pursue this angle. Club musicians often come with a unique set of challenges, but they can also be the most delightful blessing. Plus they know how to run all that sound equipment and where to find the best buys.

God may turn that "no" into a "yes" a month or a year down the road.

When you ask people, be direct: Share the vision with them and let them know what you would expect from them. It's OK if they say no, but try to stay in touch with them. Ministry is always about being in relationship with people. God may turn that "no" into a "yes" a month or a year down the road.

Another big question is this: Do you pay the musicians? There is no clear answer that fits all situations. However, experience suggests that you not pay musicians unless playing music is how they make their living. Volunteers tend to be more committed to the vision, but if you find gifted professional musicians who are committed, by all means pay them. They can be worth their weight in gold. Also, buy guitar strings, drumsticks, and so forth for your volunteers. This is a lot less expensive then paying them, and it tells them that they are appreciated.

Putting it together

Now that you have the beginnings of your team, what do you do? Hopefully you have three to six months before your first worship service to prepare. Select twenty to forty songs to build the foundation of your music library. When selecting these songs make sure the difficulty level matches the skill level of the team. Also be sure the songs aren't too difficult for congregational singing.

Effective rehearsal strategies. The most effective way to rehearse your worship team will depend in part on the size of your team. For example, if you have six instrumentalists and eight singers, you will want to split the rehearsal time if possible. There are several ways to do this. You can rehearse the musicians and singers on different nights and then do a run-through as a group an hour before your worship service. Or rehearse the whole team on the same night, splitting the team up for the first half of the rehearsal in different rooms and then bringing them all together at the end.

Find a balance between work and fun. Find a way that works best for your team. If you have a smaller group (for instance, a keyboard player, a drummer and three singers), go ahead and rehearse them all together. Another important strategy is to find a balance between work and fun. Everyone wants to do a good job, but it can't be all hard work.

Feeding the crew

Every crew needs a balanced diet to be strong and healthy. The three main spiritual food groups for a worship team are fellowship, Bible study, and sharing. This is a part of the spiritual journey that seems to happen either by chance or not at all.

At every rehearsal dedicate at least thirty minutes to feeding the crew. Fellowship will usually happen on its own before and after the rehearsal but you will need to be more intentional about the Bible study and sharing time, whether it's at the beginning, in the middle, or at the end. You can do any Bible study. One approach that works well is to study the scriptures that inspired the music you have selected. This study can help them to perform the music with more conviction.

When it comes to personal sharing and mutual support, simply give people a chance to talk about what's happening in their lives. Some people

---

While writing this chapter, I was sitting in a restaurant with my notes spread out on the table. My waitress must have seen what I was working on because she asked me if I was a worship leader. She told me that she had sung with a couple of praise teams. Thinking this was no coincidence, I asked her a few questions about what motivated her to commit to a team. The biggest motivator for her was friendship. It is great to get together with friends and make music for the Lord. —*Tom Frodsham* call this sharing "Bummers and Blessings." This is a difficult priority to keep because there never seems to be enough time to rehearse the music. But it is a great weekly reminder to us about why we are there and who really makes it happen. If you have never done this before, it will be awkward at first. But it does get easier and your team will grow in ways you never dreamed of. It all comes back to love: love of God and love of one another. "If I speak in the tongues of mortals and of angels, but have not love, I am a noisy gong or a clanging cymbal" (1 Corinthians 13:1).

Study the scriptures that inspired the music you have selected.

Support crew

The invisible giants of worship are the office administrator, office volunteers, and audiovisual technicians. These people will help you more than you can imagine and yet they can be almost invisible, which makes it very easy to forget them. These are the people who make sure all that wonderful music your team worked on actually makes it into the worship folder. They do the photocopying for you—after you have secured the necessary copyright permissions, of course! They make sure the sound is balanced right. They let you know when your keyboard player calls-in sick. They are the unsung heroes of the worship team. Be sure to thank them. They don't get the accolades the rest of the team gets; in fact, they probably only will be noticed only when they make mistakes—it's the nature of their work. Drop them a note, take them out to lunch, and regularly remind them of how important they are to this ministry.

Music

Music is the rigging for this adventure in spiritual sailing, and so building your music library and database are crucial. Doing it legally is a must. On the accompanying CD-ROM you will find helpful tools for getting organized.

See CD Resources 8A and 8B

Setting sail

Soon you will be setting sail; some already have. Along the way, there may be stormy seas or shallow waters. Sometimes you may feel like you have a mutiny on your hands. There will be days when it seems there is no wind to fill your sails and other times when the Holy Spirit will blow so hard, you can't keep up. But through it all, enjoy the journey and have fun along the way. Never take yourself too seriously. It is an important work we are called to. But in the end, who really makes it happen—God or us? If we are willing, God will use us to accomplish his purposes. This journey is a great opportunity to increase our faith, to trust God and his timing. If we can let go of our own need to control every situation, God will share with us a great adventure.

CHAPTER 9

Sound Systems and Multimedia Considerations

Ralph Sappington

I t's Sunday afternoon, the morning services went well, and you are
dozing on the couch. Like many music ministers and worship leaders,
you begin to have those familiar nightmares. You know the ones: illustrat-
ed sermons with slides that never seem to work; Christmas programs where
the kids' voices elude the microphones and parents glare at you with a dis-
dain reserved for mass murderers and puppy snatchers. Terrified, you jump
to your feet, sweat dripping from your brow, determined to never sleep
again. You think that maybe then you will escape these horrible dreams.

This chapter is intended to help you enjoy that Sunday nap and to ensure
a good night's sleep, free from sound-system nightmares and multimedia
terror. This chapter addresses worship space and the placement of speakers,
mixing boards, screens, projectors, and lights that will best serve your worshiping community. Resources on the accompanying CD-ROM will aid in
your planning, help flatten the sound-system learning curve, and define the
many new terms that you will find in this chapter.

---

*Ralph Sappington serves as minister of music at American Lutheran
Church, Billings, Montana, and adjunct instructor of music at Rocky
Mountain College.*

What do you need in a sound system?

Because you are reading this chapter, the assumption is that almost everyone in your congregation and in congregational leadership already agrees you need a sound system for your congregation, or they agree the current system is not adequate for the congregation's worship needs.

If your space has a balcony, this will add to your challenge.

To get a clear picture of what you need, begin by assessing your worship space. If you have floor plans, you are already equipped with the physical dimensions of the worship space. If there are mechanical drawings available, you can see what conduit and wiring is already in place. Also, find out what paint mixture is being used in the interior of the space and, if there is carpet, the brand and style. This will help you later in making the installation of the sound system as invisible as possible.

Next, gather everyone involved with worship and worship planning to discuss both current audiovisual needs and future dreams. Listen carefully to everyone's ideas. Planning carefully will save time and money in the future. Use the CD Resource 9A, "Sound-System Planning Sheet," to determine (1) the number and type of microphones and direct inputs needed and (2) the number of outputs required. After finishing this sheet you will also know the size of the mixing board you will need.

What do you have to work with?

See CD
Resources

Now, take a tour of the worship space. Answer all of the questions on CD Resource 9B, "Worship Space Checklist," and use "Diagram of Worship Space," CD Resource 9C. Make copies of the floor plan drawings and make notations of where the current sound system is installed. Include all microphone jacks. If you plan to have a multimedia projection system, decide where the best sight line for a screen or screens would be. At this point, take into account if there is a cross, altar, or other worship-related items that would be obscured by screens. If any of these questions are answered with a "yes," don't even think of putting the screens there, unless you are looking for a career change!

The next thing to consider is speaker placement. The two popular speaker configurations for a worship space are the center cluster and left-right placement. CD Resources 9D and 9E, "Speaker Placement Chart," will show you how important mounting and aiming the speakers is. If your space has a balcony, this will add to your challenge. The bottom line is if you use the center speaker array, you will need at least four speakers to cover the average space. Left-right placement will need a minimum of two speakers and perhaps four to cover the average worship space. You will need at least two power amps and as many as four to power your speakers.

The other major placement issue to consider is the mixing board. In many older sound installations, the mixers and power amps will be found in a closet in the very back of the worship space, locked in a cabinet. With the often complicated sound-system demands during worship these days, the mixing board needs to be in a location where the operator can respond quickly.

The best placement will be on the main floor of your space, slightly off-center. In a worship space as opposed to a concert hall, this position would be a distraction to those seated behind the console. If there is not a balcony in your space, positioning the board at the back of the room, slightly off center, will work. Under no circumstances should the sound console be placed under the balcony overhang. The operators will get a muted sound from that perspective and will have a tendency to overcompensate by pushing the high end and the overall volume. You can install the mixing board in the balcony—just make certain if you use a balcony position that you are not against a wall and that you are off-center. The reason not to center the mixing board dead center is to avoid "phase cancellation" (see page 105 in the glossary at the end of this chapter) between the side speakers.

One other important point is that you will not be helping yourself by trying to use existing sound equipment. Remember the new wine in old wineskins story (Matthew 9:17; Mark 2:22; Luke 5:37-39)? It is multiplied by infinity when it comes to sound systems.

See CD Resource 9E

Defining the project

Before you get discouraged or at best confused, take all of this information and sit down with everyone involved—pastor, worship planners, building and facilities people—and ask these questions, "Is this a project we can do ourselves? Or do we need an outside consultant to work with us? Or perhaps we need to turn it over to a sound-system professional?"

The work you have done to this point will not be in vain if you bring in a professional. You will have firsthand knowledge of the project and be equipped to oversee all aspects of your project. Your decision will be informed by the size and construction dynamics of your worship space. If you have a traditional worship space with high vaulted ceilings that would make speaker placement difficult or impossible (only ladders and volunteer muscles at your disposal), you will save time, money, and frustration by bringing in a professional. Or if there is no existing conduit available and long runs of wiring will be required, hiring a professional may also be the best decision.

Under no circumstances should the sound console be placed under the balcony overhang.

But if you have a smaller room with a flat ceiling, perhaps with acoustic tiles, and you have volunteers in your church with electrical and carpenter skills, then you have the information needed to do a professional job at a fraction of the cost. Some large music retailers have sound-system designers on staff that can take the information you have compiled and design a system for your worship space. They will ship it to you ready to install.

Fine-tuning the project

If you are going to use a consultant, think about how to choose the best person for the job. If you live in an area large enough to have several companies to choose from, you can ask for bids and proposals from the companies that other congregations have recommended. If you are in a smaller area, you will need to do some research. Get on the telephone and call other churches to get leads on finding a consultant or company that meets your needs. Ask for references and copies of proposals that the consultants have presented to other clients. Be cautious of companies that will do the installation only if they sell you the equipment. Don't be afraid to invite several companies and ask them to propose several variations of a sound system for your church.

Conquering the sound-system learning curve

With or without a consultant, this is the time to separate true needs from dreams. Ask hard questions about your real need for equipment, and place yourself in the position of defending your choices. Educate yourself on the basics of a sound system using the microphone, mixing board, and accessories fact and usage sheets on the CD-ROM.

Recording devices

If you are going to broadcast or reproduce your worship services, you will need to record them first. Just a few years ago cassette tape recorders would be the only realistic option, but with the advent of affordable digital recording devices you no longer need to put up with the hiss and poor quality of the cassette tape. For well under $1,000 you can use a mini-disk recorder, a digital audiotape (DAT) recorder, or a CD recorder. If you make tapes right after the worship service the CD recorder would be a valuable tool. A DAT recorder will record up to two hours on a small tape and a mini-disk recorder can store seventy-four minutes on a small floppy disk. All of the digital devices have affordable media.

Educate yourself on the basics of a sound system.

What about multimedia?

The very mention of large screens in worship will elicit strong responses both pro and con. Some people cannot imagine worship without the hymnal and find the projection screens a distraction to worship, while others find the freedom from keeping their eyes on a hand-held printed medium essential to worship. In our postliterate, media-intensive society, people are making their congregation choices based upon the congregation's use of media. If you are interested in attracting and keeping people from a wide range of worship experiences and getting your evangelism message across to a multisensory, stimulated audience, sooner or later you will need to address this issue.

If you have a traditional worship space with vaulted ceilings and a traditional altar area, you will need to use care in making the screen systems "invisible." This will cost more than the installation in a contemporary space but will be worth the cost in return for the support you will get from the traditional worshiping community.

First, on a 1 to 10 scale of difficulty, this is an 8.5! You should be consulting with a professional, even if you are doing the sound yourself.

The very
mention of
large screens
in worship will
elicit strong
responses.

Projection systems come in two formats—front projection and rear projection. Front projection is easier to set up but you need powerful projectors if you have a long distance from screen to projector. Rear projection can eliminate the distance of the "throw" (see page 105 in the glossary) but poses the problem of needing an enclosed area for the projectors behind the screen. Rear projection cuts down on light dimming the projected image; front projection is susceptible to outside light sources making your projection washed out.

If you find a center screen will work in your space, you have an easier job than if you need to mount your screens on each side of the room. Rear projection requires room behind the screens for an enclosed space for the projector(s). If such a space is not available, you will need to use front projection. The needed projector power is determined by the distance from projector to screen.

You will need a computer with Microsoft® PowerPoint® or a similar program installed. The computer should be located near the soundboard so you can utilize your sound person to operate the computer. A desktop computer can be used, but it would be wise to invest in a laptop so that your worship could be portable and the computer can have a second life when not used for worship.

Sharing the plans

Be prepared to meet with congregational decision-making bodies by having a copy for each member of (1) the proposal, (2) the bid, and (3) specification sheets for the equipment proposed. Use the knowledge you have gained while doing the research for the project. Check all of the prices in the bid with other sound retailers, both local and national. Have referrals from other congregations that have used the professionals you have chosen. Have photos from congregations that are similar in design to yours, portraying a visually pleasing installation and one that honors the existing architecture. Be ready to articulate how the system will be able to greatly aid and improve your congregation's worship. Keep your presentation factual, and keep it friendly and light even in the face of opposition.

Gathering the forces

Your core group of volunteers will come from your personal interaction with members of the congregation during the planning process. Count on them to be an ongoing part of this ministry, and always refer to it as ministry! Keep them informed about every step of the process. If the congregation is doing some or all of the work itself, they will be a valuable part of the work crew. Having a crew of operators who know at least how the system is put together will pay dividends when they are behind the board during a worship service or concert.

When it comes to operating the system for worship, you probably will need to develop a team that is large enough so that each member is not called upon more than once a month. Any more than that and it becomes a job; any less and your team will be rusty and unsure once behind the equipment.

Overseeing the installation

This will be a vital part of your job, if the congregation is doing all the work or if you are using a professional crew. Keep your bid sheets handy and check all components as they are installed. Any deviation from the bid should be approved by you. There will be changes due to availability, but make sure that the changes comply to your needs. Make sure all wiring is new and that more than the required lengths are used. This will come in handy if any moving of the wiring is needed at a later time.

Before you sign off on the job, every aspect of the installation should be tested and the sound system should be operating without feedback, buzzes, humming, or snap, crackle, and pop sounds! Require that the installers be present when you train your volunteer team.

Training multimedia volunteers

It is critical that everyone who might be called upon to turn on the system complete a hands-on training session. Begin your training session with a walking tour of the multimedia system. Make sure everyone knows where the power amplifiers and the breaker boxes are located. The next stop would be the microphone and instrument inputs. Plug and unplug a mike to see how a good connection feels. Inspect a "direct box" (see page 104 in the glossary) and become familiar with the polarity options. This will be important if a guitar or other instrument has a buzz.

Every aspect of the installation should be tested.

Provide a layout of your sound system and photocopy a mixing board layout from the manual that came with your board. This way all of your operators know how the system is laid out so that any problem can be traced more quickly. The mixing console layout will allow them to see where the sound is going; if it's not getting where it should be, they can find the problem.

Rehearsing a service

After the system is installed, gather your sound team, musicians, and pastors. Using the Sunday morning worship folder, go through each section of the service. Make sure all of the mikes are live and picking up the speakers and singers. Be certain that everyone can hear the monitors and that the monitors are not overpowering the house sound. If you are using multimedia, make sure your operators can follow the cues for slide changes and still keep track of the sound requirements. Let each of the operators have a chance with each section of the service. Remember, there is no better way to learn than to do!

A weekly run-through might save you from Sunday morning disasters. Using the worship folder for Sunday morning, get the operators for that weekend together and check all the microphones that will be used in the worship service. Mark the folder as to when to have them live and when to mute them. If you are using PowerPoint or something similar, view each slide carefully and make sure the slide matches the reference in the worship folder. Check the slides for typos. Taking this one hour a week will insure that your volunteers will feel confident about their job and that worship can take place without any distractions.

Remaining details

Once your sound system and multimedia system are in place, make sure you have a safe and secure place to store mikes and other small items between services and that everyone knows how to power down your system to avoid damage to the system. If you can keep the mixing board out of reach when not in use, do it! Otherwise prepare a sheet noting all of the settings and double check it before turning the system on. This will save you from enduring the feedback howl that comes when a three-year-old discovers how fun it is to move sliders on a mixing board up and down and up and . . . You get the picture. Know what it will take to maintain the system and keep a supply of extra mike cables, mike clips and fuses handy. The odds are you won't need them unless you don't have them!

Now, lie down and take that nap. You deserve it! You can rest easy, knowing that everything is in order for the next worship service.

See the glossary of common sound-system terms on pages 104-105.

A weekly run-through prevents Sunday morning disasters.

Glossary

Definitions of common sound-system terms

See CD
Resource
9F

Analog. Meaning "just like" but not "exactly the same." The tape stores a replica of the sound, not a duplicate. See *Digital*.

Aux In. An input on the mixing board that allows an effect to be sent to selected channels.

Aux Out. An output on the mixing board that allows a selected channels signal to be sent out of the board.

Buses. An output that will carry a number of channels out of the mixing board.

Canon Connector. The three-prong plug found on microphones.

Channel. An input on the mixing board that allows you to manipulate the sound assigned to that channel.

Compression. An effect that controls the range of volume by limiting the louds and increasing the softs.

Delay Amps. Amplifiers that delay the sound so that it reaches the front and the back of a room at the same time.

Digital. Meaning "exactly the same." Digital recording stores a duplicate of the sound.

Direct Box. A box that allows a guitar (or other instrument) chord to be sent to the board by way of a *Microphone Cable*.

Direct Inputs. Inputs on your board that bypass everything and go directly to the *Outputs*.

Distortion. A bad sound that occurs on the sound system when the volume exceeds the amplifier's ability to handle the sound. Good for guitars!

Doubly. Same as *Dolby*. A noise-reduction tool used in analog recording. Rent the movie *This Is Spinal Tap*.

Effects Units. A unit that connects to your auxiliaries to supply a variety of effects to a sound—reverb, delay, and others.

EQ. *Equalization*. The ability to change the sound by increasing and decreasing frequencies.

Faders. The sliding knobs that control volume on a mixing board.

Feedback. Your worst nightmare! The high-pitched sound that will turn into a deafening roar if not controlled. See *EQ*.

Ground Loop. A hum caused by the polarity of a power cord or input being different than the other cords or inputs.

Grounding. A ground can be any wire attached to a nonconductive item.

Headroom. The distance between the volume of your system and the system's ability to produce volume.

High Gain. A nongrounded input that only accepts a cable with positive and negative connectors.

Input Gain. A knob on the mixing board that adjusts the strength of signal going into the board.

Inputs. The connections on the back of your board where you plug stuff in.

Instrument Cable. A cable that only has two wires in it. Used for guitars and keyboards. See *High Gain*.

Leader. On cassette tapes, the white part you can't record on. (Otherwise, it's the person to blame when things go wrong.)

Low Gain. A grounded input that accepts positive, negative, and ground cables. See *Canon Connectors.*

Mains. The main speakers or the fader that controls them.

Microphone Cable. *See* Canon Connectors.

Mix. The final output of your system.

Mixing Board. The unit that accepts all of the signals and sends out the mix.

Monitors. The speakers that allow the singers, instrumentalists, and presenters to hear the sound.

Mono. One signal going out. Even if you have a left and right output, the signal is the same.

Mute. A handy switch that turns off the sound.

Outputs. Any connection that provides sound going out.

Pad. See *Input Gain.*

Pan. A knob that allows you to send a signal left or right in the mix.

Phase Cancellation. When two signals collide in the air and reduce the combined volume—a bad thing.

Polarity. Like the battery cable in your car, the positive and negative need to be the same.

Post Fader. A sound that will be affected by the moving of its channel fader.

Pots. Also known as knobs.

Power Amps. The amplifiers that provide power to the speakers.

Prefader. A sound that will not be affected by the movement of its channel fader.

Quarter-Inch Cable. See *Instrument Cable.*

Returns. If you send a signal out, this is where it comes back into your board. See *Aux In.*

Reverb. An effect that adds the "echo" sound. It also occurs without assistance in large rooms.

RF Interference. *Radio frequency interference* that often affects wireless mikes, causing noise and unwanted input.

Sends. See *Outputs.*

Sliders. See *Faders.*

Solo. A switch that allows you to hear one channel without affecting the total output of the board.

Speaker Array. Any grouping of speakers.

Speaker Cable. A nonshielded cable that carries sound to the speakers.

Stereo. The ability to send two signals out, left and right.

Sub Woofer. A speaker that provides the very low sounds. Often used in cars to produce the "thump."

Thingy. A term for any button, box, or knob that is not labeled and you have no idea what it's really called.

Throw. The distance the light or sound travels until its reaches its target.

Tweeter. A speaker that provides the very high sounds.

Whatyoucallit. See *Thingy.*

Woofer. The speaker that provides the "middle" sounds.

XLR Plug. See *Canon Connector.*

Resource List

Books

Postmodern culture and the church

Aqua Church, Leonard Sweet. Loveland, Col.: Group, 1999.

Beyond Foundationalism: Shaping Theology in a Postmodern Context, Stanley J. Grenz and John Franke. Grand Rapids, Mich.: Eerdmans, 2000.

The Church on the Other Side, Brian D. McLaren. Grand Rapids, Mich.: Zondervan, 1998.

ChurchNext: Quantum Changes in How We Do Ministry, Eddie Gibbs. Downer's Grove, Ill.: InterVarsity Press, 2000.

The End of the World . . . As We Know It, Chuck Smith Jr. Colorado Springs, Col.: WaterBrook Press, 2000.

The Experience Economy, B. J. Pine and J. H. Gilmore. Boston: Harvard Business School Press, 1999.

Generating Hope: A Strategy for Reaching the Postmodern Generation, Jimmy Long. Downer's Grove, Ill.: InterVarsity Press, 1997.

Getting Real: An Interactive Guide to Relational Ministry, Ken Baugh and Rich Hurst. Colorado Springs, Col.: NavPress, 2000.

A Primer on Postmodernism, Stanley J. Grenz. Grand Rapids, Mich.: Eerdmans, 1996.

Postmodern Pilgrims, Leonard Sweet. Nashville: Broadman and Holman, 2000.

Power Surge, Michael Foss. Minneapolis: Augsburg Fortress, 2000.

Soul Tsunami, Leonard Sweet. Grand Rapids, Mich.: Zondervan, 1999.

Threshold of the Future: Reforming the Church in the Post-Christian West, Michael Riddell. SPCK, 1998.

Truth Is Stranger than It Used to Be: Biblical Faith in a Postmodern Age, Richard Middleton and Brian Walsh. Downer's Grove, Ill.: InterVarsity Press, 1995.

Virtual Faith: The Irreverent Spiritual Quest of Generation X, Tom Beaudoin. San Francisco: Jossey-Bass, 1998.

What Next? Connecting Your Ministry with the Generation Formerly Known as X, Janet M. Corpus, Pam Fickenscher, Michael Housholder, Mark A. Peterson, Christine L. Reifschneider, and Richard Webb. Minneapolis: Augsburg Fortress, 1999.

Worship issues and planning

Blended Worship, Robert E. Webber. Peabody, Mass.: Hendrickson, 1994.

Calendar: Christ's Time for the Church, Laurence Hill Stookey. Nashville: Abingdon, 1996.

Guide to Sound Systems for Worship, Jon Eiche. Milwaukee, Wis.: Hal Leonard Publishing, 1990.

Handbook for Multisensory Worship, Kim Miller and Ginghamsburg UMC Worship Team. Nashville: Abingdon, 1999.

The New Worship, Barry Liesch. Baker, 1996.

NIV Worship Bible, Buddy Owens, ed. Washington, D.C.: Maranatha, 2000.

Out on the Edge, Michael Slaughter. Nashville: Abingdon, 1998.

Planning Blended Worship, Robert E. Webber. Nashville: Abingdon, 1998.

The Praise and Worship Bible. Wheaton, Ill.: Tyndale, 1999.

Sundays and Seasons (annual resource). Minneapolis: Augsburg Fortress.

United Methodist Music and Worship Planner. Nashville: Abingdon, 2000.

Worship Evangelism, Sally Morgenthaler. Grand Rapids, Mich.: Zondervan, 1995.

Art

Art and Soul: Signposts for Christians in the Arts, Hilary Brand and Adrienne Chaplin. Solway/Paternoster, 1999.

The Psalms: An Artist's Interpretation, Eugene Peterson and Anneka Kaai. Downer's Grove, Ill.: InterVarsity, 2000.

The Source Resource Guide for Using Creative Arts in Church Services, Scott Dyer and Nancy Beach. Grand Rapids, Mich.: Zondervan, 1996.

Readings and drama

Can These Bones Live? Contemporary Dramas for Lent and Easter, David H. Kehret. Minneapolis: Augsburg Fortress, 1999.

A Cry Like a Bell: Poems of Human Struggle and God's Grace, Madeleine L'Engle. Wheaton, Ill.: Harold Shaw Publishers, 1987.

Leading in Prayer: A Workbook for Worship, Hughes Oliphant Old. Grand Rapids, Mich.: Eerdmans, 1995.

The One Year Book of Poetry: 365 Devotional Readings Based on Classic Christian Verse, Phillip Comfort and Daniel Partner. Wheaton, Ill.: Tyndale House, 1999.

Scripture Out Loud! Dramatic Readings for Lent and Easter, Marianne Houle and Jeffrey Phillips. Minneapolis: Augsburg Fortress, 1999.

Worship music

The Best of the Best in Contemporary Christian Music, Mike Zehnder, ed. Tempe, Ariz.: Fellowship Ministries, 2000.

Choosing Contemporary Music, Terri Bocklund McLean and Rob Glover, compilers. Minneapolis: Augsburg Fortress, 2000.

Leading the Church's Song, Robert Buckley Farlee, ed. Minneapolis: Augsburg Fortress, 1998.

New Harmonies, Terri Bocklund McLean. Bethesda, Md.: Alban, 1998.

One Body, Alive! (CD). Minneapolis: Augsburg Fortress, 2000.

Worship and Praise Songbook. Minneapolis: Augsburg Fortress, 1999.

Music technique

Contemporary Music Styles, Robert Barrett, 1996.

Reading and Writing Chord Charts, Robert Barrett, 1998.

Story

The Book of God: The Bible as Novel, Walter Wangerin Jr. Grand Rapids, Mich.: Zondervan, 1996.

The Book That Reads Me, Hans-ruedi Weber. New York: World Council of Churches Publications, 1995.

Preparing for Jesus: Meditations on the Coming of Christ, Advent, Christmas and the Kingdom, Walter Wangerin Jr. Grand Rapids, Mich.: Zondervan, 1999.

Reliving the Passion: Meditations on the Death and Resurrection of Jesus, Walter Wangerin Jr. Grand Rapids, Mich.: Zondervan, 1992.

The Storyteller's Companion to the Bible (ten volumes). Nashville: Abingdon, 1996.

Magazines

General worship

Beyond Magazine
 (www.beyondmag.com)

Christianity and the Arts
 (www.christianarts.net)

The Crossing: Christian Arts
 Newsletter
 (www.promontoryartists.org/
 crossing)

Cutting Edge

Echo

The Edge
 (www.youth.co.za/theedge)

Faithworks (www.faithworks.com)

FutureWorship
 (www.futureworship.com)

Image Arts (www.imagejournal.org)

Next Wave (www.next-wave.org)

The Ooze (www.theooze.com)

Re:generation
 (www.regenerator.com)

Rev. Magazine
 (TheRev@Rev-Magazine.com)

Worship Leader
 (www.worshipleader.org).
 See "The Church Electric,"
 Summer 2000.

Sermon preparation

The Clergy Journal. Lectionary-
based sermons for every Sunday
and Holy Day of the year. P.O.
Box 240, South St. Paul, MN
55075.

Emphasis. Similar in format to
Pulpit Resource. 517 S. Main St.,
P.O. Box 4503, Lima, OH 45802.

Pulpit Resource. Exegetical and
illustration material for the
common lectionary readings.
6160 Carmen Ave. E., Inver Grove
Heights, MN 55076.

Software resources

Bible Explorer. Epiphany Software
http://www.epiphanysoftware.com.
Contains Bible translations, commentaries, dictionaries, maps, con-
cordances, and Greek and Hebrew
dictionaries. Refer to the accompanying CD Resource 6E for an
example of how "Bible Explorer"
can be used in the Bible study
phase of sermon preparation.

INFOsearch (http://infosearch.com).
Illustrations, periodical articles,
jokes, cartoons, and famous
quotations, songs, hymns, praise
choruses, and litanies catalogued
by scripture reference, topics, or
words. Reference the accompanying CD for viewable screens of

sermon illustrations and music linked to a specific Bible passage.

SongSelect. CCLI (http://www.ccli.com). A tool to select, print, and track the use of hymns and songs in worship; access to more than 150,000 songs and hymns licensed by Christian Copyright Licensing International.

WORDSearch. iExalt Electronic Publishing Company, (http://wordsearchbible.com). A complete library for personal Bible study, sermon preparation, and Bible study material preparation. Compatible with a reference collection known as STEP-compatible resources.

Web sites

Alternative-worship sites
(United States, United Kingdom, and Australia)

freshworship.org

greenbelt.org.uk

holyspace.org

mosaic.org

prodigal-project.com

sanctus.org.uk

the-mass.com

Art: religious images

clark.net/pub/webbge/jesus.htm
  (images of Jesus)

crossart.godzone.net.nz/

execpc.com/~tmuth/st_john/xmas/
  art.htm (Christmas art)

iconography.com

natcath.org
  (multicultural images of Jesus)

smc.qld.edu.au/relart.htm

Art museums

http://metalab.unc.edu/wm/
  (Web Museum)

nga.gov/search/search.htm
  (Natopmal Gallery of Art)

ocaiw.com/pintura.htm
  (classic art by artist and category)

thinker.org
  (San Francisco Museum of Art)

Congregations

Casas Adobes Baptist Church,
  Tucson, Arizona,
  www.CasasChurch.org

Community Church of Joy,
  Glendale, Arizona,
  www.joyonline.org

Flamingo Road Church,
  Fort Lauderdale, Florida,
  www.flamingoroad.org

Ginhamsburg United Methodist
  Church, Tipp City, Ohio,
  www.ginghamsburg.org

Hillsong Church,
  Sydney, Australia,
  www.hillsclc.org.au

Mars Hill Fellowship,
  Seattle, Washington,
  www.marshillchurch.org

Mosaic, Los Angeles, California,
  www.mosaic.org

Prince of Peace Lutheran Church,
  Burnsville, Minnesota,
  www.princeofpeaceonline.org and
  www.changingchurch.org

Saddleback Church,
  Lake Forest, California,
  www.saddleback.com

Willow Creek Community Church,
  South Barrington, Illinois,
  www.willowcreek.com

Windsor Village United Methodist
  Church, Houston, Texas,
  www.kingdombuilder.com

Wooddale Church,
  Eden Prairie, Minnesota,
  www.wooddale.org

Cultural trends

altculture.com

www.epictivity.com

fastcompany.com

generationjones.com

iconoculture.com

www.leonardsweet.com

journale.com/stories.html

regenerator.com

salonmagazine.com

slate.com

theatlantic.com

wired.com

Film and video

hollywoodjesus.com

osbd.org (See "Images for
  Worship 1, 2, and 3.")

Technology and resources

acousticalsolutions.com, audio

belief.net, Christian ministry and
  issues

ccli.com, music licensing

Christianity.com, Christian
  ministry and issues

christianv-a.com, film and video
  equipment

churchsoundcheck.com, audio

communityworship.com, worship
  team hymnbook

crosslife.org.nz, creative arts in
  church

www.elca.org/eteam, Web site of
  Evangelical Lutheran Church
  in America evangelism and
  discipleship ministry

www.epictivity.com, basics of
  Leonard Sweet's EPIC worship
  in Christian community

firstevan.org/articles.htm, blended
  worship, practical help

fowlerinc.com, technical products

friendsofthegroom.com, drama

homileticsonline.com,
  ministry and preaching

interlinc-online.com, privately
  distributed Christian videos

kellycarpenter.com, worship
  leading, songwriting,
  keyboard information

lightronics.com, lights

midimusic.miningco.com,
  Christian midi sites

praise.net/worship/list, on-line
  worship discussion

seekersolutions.com, general

sermonnotes.com, preaching

textweek.com, lectionary text
  ideas and links

tfwm.com, technical information

u.arizona.edu/~dpc, movies
  and worship

yourchurch.net, technical
  and general help

worshipinfo.com,
  keyboard information

worshipleader.org, worship
  leadership

Photography

arttoday.com

bizpresenter.com

corbis.com

eyewire.com

harbingeronline.com

jamphotography.com, nature and
  Christian

http://jrbell.crossdaily.com,
  John Bell's Christian Art

photolib.noaa.gov, nature photos

webshots.com

Worship music

268store.com

goldusa.com

integritymusic.com

primenet.com/~getdown

songdiscovery.com, *Worship
  Leader* magazine resource

verticalmusic.com, *Integrity
  Hosanna,* alternative worship

vineyardmusic.com

worshipinfo.com

worshipmusic.com

worshiptogether.com, EMI